GREAT HOUSES OF
CHICAGO

1871–1921

GREAT HOUSES OF
CHICAGO
1871–1921

Susan Benjamin and Stuart Cohen

Foreword by Franz Schulze and Arthur H. Miller

ACANTHUS PRESS

NEW YORK : 2008

Acanthus Press, LLC
54 West 21st Street
New York, New York 10010
www.acanthuspress.com

Library of Congress Cataloging-in-Publication Data

Benjamin, Susan S.
Great houses of Chicago, 1871-1921 / by Susan Benjamin and Stuart Cohen;
foreword by Franz Schulze and Arthur H. Miller.
p. cm. -- (Urban domestic architecture series)
Includes bibliographical references and index.
ISBN 0-926494-39-2 (alk. paper)
1. Dwellings--Illinois--Chicago. 2. Mansions--Illinois--Chicago. 3.
Historic buildings--Illinois--Chicago. 4. Architecture,
Domestic--Illinois--Chicago. 5. Chicago (Ill.)--Buildings, structures, etc.
6. Rich people--Homes and haunts--Illinois--Chicago. 7. Rich
people--Illinois--Chicago--Biography. 8. Upper
class--Illinois--Chicago--History. 9. Chicago (Ill.)--Biography. 10.
Architects--Illinois--Chicago--Biography. I. Cohen, Stuart Earl, 1942- II. Title.

F548.7.B46 2008
728.809773'1109034--dc22
2007026889

FRONTISPIECE: Main stair, Joseph T. Ryerson Jr. house, 1921. David Adler, architect.

Book design by Maggie Hinders

Printed in China

URBAN DOMESTIC ARCHITECTURE SERIES

FOR THREE HUNDRED YEARS, Americans have sought to fulfill the promise of a better life that a rich wilderness held out to the first settlers as they stepped onto the shores of the North Atlantic. The American engagement with a vast continent has been defined by the necessary development and expansion of cities and the ensuing preservation and enjoyment of a bucolic countryside.

The Acanthus Press series, Urban Domestic Architecture, presents landmark residential buildings of the last two centuries that display the innovative housing solutions of Americans and their architects as they sought the ideal domestic life.

CONTENTS

FOREWORD

SUSAN BENJAMIN AND STUART COHEN have done a tremendous service in gathering together for the first time a substantial body of images about Chicago houses from the 1870s to the 1920s. Some of this rich heritage has been hinted at in books such as David Lowe's *Lost Chicago* and *Chicago Interiors*, in books on single houses such as the Nickerson mansion or Wright's Robie house, or in guides like Jean Block's *Hyde Park Houses* (1978) or the excellent *AIA Guide to Chicago*, now in its second edition (2002). Long ago in the 1940s, John Drury performed pioneer work in his *Old Chicago Houses*, though he mostly discussed the history of the builders and inhabitants. Books on architects, as well, have been helpful for those interested in Chicago houses—including Richard Pratt's 1970 book on David Adler (now a great collector's item); Sarah B. Landau's 1981 book on Peter B. Wight; Robert Bruegmann's 1991 three-volume catalog and 1997 book, both about Holabird & Roche, Virginia Greene's 1998 book on Howard Van Doren Shaw; and the many treatments of Wright's Chicago work. But never before have so many stunning photographs of great and significant Chicago houses been made available together and in juxtaposition with one another, with useful historic and biographical context and frequently also with helpful close readings of the architecture and design. Here are almost three dozen of the best places—some treasured and preserved, some stable, and some lost—all remembered as they were when they were built and during the period covered in this study.

Surely it is one thing to see the Charnley and Robie houses discussed in the context of Sullivan's and Wright's bodies of work or Adler's Ryerson townhouses on Astor Street and Lakeview in the context of that master's contrasting stunning body of work. But to see these together in one volume along with so many of the other houses of the period, which were their peers, is illuminating indeed. The reader can join the authors in tracking the shifts in taste and style cycles from avant-garde to passé.

The authors follow several lines of dramatic tension, from the aping of European taste to attempts to define new national and regional styles and from the sturdy, dark, cluttered European-inspired interiors of the 1880s to the bright, delicate new-style rooms by the 1910s and 1920s. Certainly the World's Columbian Exposition of 1893, held here in Chicago, which had a profound influence in classicizing taste in this country for the next 50 years, can be seen influencing Chicago design traditions for commercial, public, and also domestic building. The untimely 1891 death of John Root, a champion of the organic Richardsonian vision described in the introduction, also impacted this dynamic design environment.

Here, though, the authors show the gradual shifting of taste and style from continental to a naturalizing Romanesque and then into separate branches for Colonial Revival/Greek and Roman classic, for English traditional historicism, and also for regional, Asian-influenced Prairie School. These shifts reveal themselves in the eclecticism of late-19th century and early-20th century works like the 1902 Madlener house of Schmidt and Garden, which blends Sullivan and Wright–derived ornament for stairs and stonework with some more historically-based art glass design. This rich dynamic reflected sometimes the nationalities of newer European immigrants or members of still-identifiable ethnic subcommunities. One example is found in the various Germanic tones of the Dewes and Madlener residences. The many wonderful plans displayed, as well, show these shifts in approach and taste, sometimes quite gradually, as in the 1903 modish Prairie style Rosenwald mansion with its quite traditional, even Belle Epoque, symmetrical plan, distinctly designated spaces, and even third-floor ballroom. The jump about a mile to the 1909 Robie house, in plan as well as style, then, is all the more affecting.

Did Chicago have a distinctive style or type of townhouse, as did Boston, New York, or Washington? Or as did London, Paris, or Italian cities like Rome, Florence, and Venice? Yes, but only in part: the innovative regional style of Sullivan, Wright, and Garden stood out only in a few quarters, such as Hyde Park and nearby suburbs Oak Park and River Forest. The region's geographic character prevailed upon style less than did the elite's sense of ancestral European heritage. This could be recent, as with brewers like Edward Uihlein. Or it could be more abstractly recalled in a genealogical past, as with the Anglo-Saxon and sometimes New England–descended native-born individuals who sought out, for example, the trappings of Tudor new-money feudal respectability. One such Chicagoan was meatpacker Edward Morris.

But Chicago's variously styled neighborhoods like Astor Street, North Rush Street, Prairie Avenue, and even Hyde Park/Kenwood reflected an uninhibited, distinctively American approach in that age, mostly before the income tax was restored in 1913. This was derived from an instant connection with the westward course of empire, embodied in the 1893 World's Fair, which brought Chicago recognition as a world city—following in turn the golden ages of Athens, Rome, Paris, London, Boston, and New York. In no place in the East had so much happened so quickly, with no intervening architectural stages of adolescence or callow youth. Chicago sprang onto the world stage when American architects and their clients were first experiencing Europe directly with new Pullman high-speed, overnight trains to the East Coast and regularly scheduled steamer service across the Atlantic. Perhaps in no place else in America did this shock of cultural recognition have such a profound and lasting effect as it did in Chicago from the 1870s to the 1920s. And perhaps in no other place did it lead to so many fruitful new architectural and design directions, in the city and in the North Shore suburbs already chronicled by the authors. Stuart Cohen and Susan Benjamin again are the reader's guides here to that remarkable cultural flowering, this time in the city of Chicago proper.

Franz Schulze
Arthur H. Miller

ACKNOWLEDGMENTS

IN OUR QUEST for information—history, engaging stories, and images—we are indebted to a great many people. We would like to thank all of them for their time and invaluable contributions to this book.

Arthur Miller, Archivist and Librarian for Special Collections, Lake Forest College, and Franz Schulze, the Betty Jane Schultz Hollender Professor of Art, Emeritus, Lake Forest College, not only wrote the foreword to our book, but continuously provided us with information, encouragement, and their considerable expertise. Along with Raymond "Terry" Tatum, Supervising Historian and Director of Research, Chicago Department of Planning and Development, Landmarks Division, Arthur Miller and Franz Schulze were diligent readers of our text, continually making many helpful suggestions and corrections. We wish to especially thank the Board of Trustees of the Graham Foundation for Advanced Studies in the Fine Arts for a grant that enabled us to purchase many of the fine illustrations in this book.

We also wish to thank Sarah Herda, Director, and Carolyn Kelly of the Graham Foundation for generously lending us photographs of the Madlener House; Pauline Saliga, Executive Director, Society of Architectural Historians, who wholeheartedly endorsed our efforts; Julie McKeon, for researching information for us and continuously making time to find answers to last-minute questions; Gwen Sommers Yant, who read text and provided us with many helpful suggestions; Jean Follett, who gave the text a final reading; Lesley A. Martin and Robert Medina, who helped us locate and shared with us images from the Chicago Historical Museum's invaluable photographic archive; Mary Woolever and Aimee Marshall, of the Ryerson and Burnham Libraries at the Art Institute of Chicago, who generously provided us with scanned photographs; Lori Boyer and Kim Krueger of the Architecture Department, Art Institute of Chicago, who graciously researched drawings for us; Jackie Maman, Image Licensing, Art Institute of Chicago; Daniel Meyer, Associate Curator of Special Collections and University Archivist at the University of Chicago Library, who provided us with photographs of Hyde Park houses; Lee Grady, McCormick—International Harvester Collection Archivist, Wisconsin Historical Society, for his guidance in providing us material from the McCormick family archives; Martha Briggs, Lloyd Lewis Curator of Midwest Manuscripts, Roger and Julie Baskes Department of Special Collections, Newberry Library; Corina Carusi, Curator, Glessner House Museum, for all her help with Prairie Avenue research and new information on the Glessner House; Susan Perry, Architectural Historian, Chicago Department of Planning and

Development, Landmarks Division, for the hours she spent providing us with information on Chicago Landmarks; Dr. M. Kirby Talley, Jr., Director, The Richard H. Driehaus Museum, for his guidance in researching the Nickerson House; William Tyre, SAH Comptroller and Manager of Programs, Charnley-Persky House Museum, for providing us with information and photographs of Prairie Avenue and the Gold Coast; Lauren Finch and Ted Cueller of the Frank Lloyd Wright Preservation Trust, for photographs of the Robie House; Rebecca Price, special collections of the Art, Architecture & Engineering Library of the University of Michigan, for photographs of the Robie House; Susan K. Rishworth, Archivist at the American College of Surgeons, for providing us with photographs of the Nickerson House; Mari Nakahara, archivist at the Prints & Drawings Collection, the Octagon, the Museum of the American Architectural Foundation, for access to their Richard Morris Hunt collection; John Graf, the author of *Chicago's Mansions*, who lent us the image of the Carter Harrison house from his private collection; Francis Cardinal George, OMI, Archbishop of Chicago, who generously granted us permission to include the Archbishop's Residence in our book; John J. Treanor, Vice Chancellor, and Peggy O' Toole, Chief Processing Archivist, Archdiocese of Chicago's Joseph Cardinal Bernardin Archives and Record Center, who provided us with original drawings of the Archbishop's Residence and arranged for interior photography of the residence for inclusion in our book. Historic drawings were provided by Jim Nagle of Nagle Hartray Danker Kagan McKay Penney Architects Ltd., who were the architects for the conversion of the Patterson house to condominiums; David Seglin, architect for the conversion of the Isham Mansion to condominiums, supplied information; John Eifler, the project architect for Skidmore, Owings and & Merrill's restoration of the Charnley house, provided us with floor plans. Thanks to John Vinci, for allowing us to use the beautiful drawings he prepared of the Glessner house and his floor plans of the Madlener house; Don Phillips of Stuart Cohen & Julie Hacker Architects LLC, who redrew plans of the Goodman and MacVeagh houses for use in our book; Robin Goldsmith, Jane Dickson, and Mary Shea, who spent considerable time providing us with information on the history of the Fortnightly and read our essay on the Lathrop House, home to the Fortnightly; Stephen Salny, whose impeccable research on David Adler was a constant source of information and encouragement; John Notz, for generously providing us with information on the Uihlein family; Linda Liang, who aided with extensive primary research on the McCormick family; Betty Blum, who gave us background on the Blatchford family that enabled us to include the house in our book; Louise More of the Blatchford family, who provided us with stunning photographs of her grandfather's house; Melinda Kwedar, Kenilworth Historical Society; Kathleen Roy Cummings, whose information on George Maher proved invaluable; Julia Johnas, Highland Park Public Library, generously answered questions; Elaine Coorens, whose research on the Wicker Park neighborhood has been enormously helpful; Beverly Siegel, who taught us the importance of Julius Rosenwald; Edmund Gronkiewicz, Martin and Ursula von Walterskirschen, Bunny Gallagher, Joe Howard, Jan Miller, Carol Wyant, and Liz O'Brien; Julie and Fred Lasko, the owners of the Dewes house, who provided us with several photographs; Jennifer Kenny; Paul Lane of Photo Source, Evanston, who scanned many of the images in our book; and Nan Greenough, who was a constant source of advice and encouragement. Our thanks to Mary Alice Molloy, not only for her study of Prairie Avenue, but for information on Richardson's MacVeagh house, which she so generously shared, and to all the scholars of architecture and Chicago's social and cultural history whose research and writing enabled us to think through and work out our ideas for the book.

Although it was the publisher's intention that the houses in this book be portrayed by archival photography, this book contains some contemporary photographs of important extant buildings where no interior photography either existed or survived. We are indebted to Howard Kaplan for his beautiful photographs of the Fortnightly and to Tina Leto, the Archdiocese of Chicago's photographer, for her stunning interior pictures of the Archbishop's Residence. We have also used the Hedrich Blessing photographs taken by Nick Merrick of the Charnley house just after its restoration.

Because photographs and drawings could not always be found, especially of Chicago's early residences, it was impossible to include many of the city's great houses in our book. Architects, historians, and homeowners generously suggested buildings we hoped to include, but many of these houses were neither photographed nor published and are sadly now gone. Although, with great help, we uncovered numerous spectacular photographs, it is our profound wish that we could have located still more of the often-elusive images.

We want to personally thank Barry Cenower, our editor and publisher, for his enthusiastic encouragement and help in narrowing down an overwhelming amount of information and images, a task which he attacked with patience and impartiality. We wish to acknowledge our mentors, William Jordy (Susan) and Colin Rowe (Stuart), who cultivated the analytical and visual skills that made this book possible. We especially want to thank Susan's husband, Wayne, and Stuart's wife, Julie Hacker, and our children, Michael, Jennie, and David Benjamin and Gabriel Cohen, who never complained, offered continuous support, and were never upset when we ventured out to investigate Chicago's amazing architectural resources or sequestered ourselves to write.

LAKE SHORE DRIVE LOOKING NORTH, 1926

GREAT HOUSES: THE CHICAGO STORY

P OETRY PORTRAYS CHICAGO far better than does prose. The city's most famous bard, Carl Sandburg, characterized late 19th-century Chicago more authentically and eloquently than any historian:

> *Hog Butcher for the World*
> *Tool Maker, Stacker of Wheat*
> *Player with Railroads and the Nation's Freight Handler;*
> *Stormy, husky, brawling*
> *City of the Big Shoulders*

"CHICAGO," CARL SANDBURG, 1916

Chicago's great houses were built by entrepreneurs who gave the growing metropolis its worldwide reputation as the City of the Big Shoulders. It was a place where Europeans, New Englanders, New Yorkers, southerners, and nearby midwesterners migrated to make their way—more specifically, to make their fortunes. From meager beginnings, men created enormously successful businesses: Philip D. Armour and Gustavus Swift in meatpacking; Cyrus McCormick and John J. Glessner in farm implements; Montgomery Ward, Richard Sears, and Julius Rosenwald in the mail-order business; George Pullman in railroading; Marshall Field in dry goods; and Potter Palmer as a retailer, hotelier, and real-estate developer. The houses they built became the physical embodiment of their accomplishments.

Chicago was a compelling destination. Because of its strategic location, the pioneers who settled on the swampy land at the edge of America's central inland sea envisioned a place of unlimited potential. Even its name was auspicious. Legends abound relating to its derivation, but *Chicago* is generally thought to derive from a Native American word meaning "wild onion," which some writers believe correlates with the city's strength. From a frontier settlement incorporated as a town in 1833 with a population of 350 residents in an area only three-eighths of a mile square, Chicago grew by 1860 into a city with a population of 109,263. And the phenomenal growth continued, fulfilling the potential of the city's location, in the middle of the country at the confluence of Lake Michigan and the Chicago River and surrounded by the world's most productive agricultural land. Chicago became not only the

HENRY B. "WIDOW" CLARKE HOUSE, 1836

largest grain and lumber market in the United States, but also the country's transportation hub. Freight cars and steamboats carried raw goods into the city and delivered finished products to points throughout the United States.

The vitality of Chicago and the enterprising spirit of its successful residents were captured in a book on Chicago written in 1917 by H. C. Chatfield-Taylor. He grew up on the west side of Chicago, the son of an agricultural-machinery manufacturer who had amassed a huge fortune through hard work and astute real-estate investments. Chatfield-Taylor characterized Chicago as "a city without idlers." He described his town as "one huge kettle of energy

seething the whole day long, no healthy man or woman being able to exist without work of some kind or other to do." He saw Chicago as "the stupendous product of the pioneer spirit."

Chicago's pioneer entrepreneurs and their children hired prestigious architects to design new houses, or they bought and remodeled existing ones. As their wealth increased, families moved to more fashionable neighborhoods. Novelist Arthur Meeker Jr., who grew up on posh Prairie Avenue in a house that his family remodeled and then lived in for 11 years, recalled that Chicagoans moved perpetually. When people outgrew their quarters, he said, they restlessly

CARTER HARRISON HOUSE, 1858

looked for something better. The Meekers' Prairie Avenue house was the third his parents occupied when they moved back to Chicago from London, where his father managed Armour & Company's European operation. When Prairie Avenue became unfashionable, the senior Meeker, along with J. Ogden Armour, purchased property across from Lincoln Park. Their move made the area north of the Gold Coast desirable.

Chicago's oldest documented residence (and the city's only remaining example of Greek Revival architecture) is the Henry B. Clarke house. Built in 1836, it was the largest house on the south side, originally located on 20 acres near Wabash and 18th Street. Clarke, who came from New York State, was a self-made man. He established a prosperous hardware business and became one of the town's leading citizens. His first family house was a temporary log structure, but when he acquired sufficient money, he replaced it with an imposing Greek Revival mansion, on land sufficient for leading the life of a country squire. Although he died in the cholera epidemic of 1849, his wife remained in the residence, and the place is sometimes referred to as the Widow Clarke House. After the great fire of 1871, the Clarke house (which had survived the disaster) was purchased by John Chrimes, a prominent Chicago tailor.

Fearing a recurrence of the fire, he had the structure moved farther south to 45th Street. Over the years, the house became rundown and lost its front portico. In 1977, it was again moved, this time to its original location. The Clarke residence has been restored and is open to the public as a house museum.

As the city grew during the late 1850s and the 1860s, Chicago's west side attracted many successful businessmen. Elegant mansions and townhouses lined Ashland Avenue and Washington and Warren boulevards. The west-side residents who occupied these houses included Scotsman Allan Pinkerton, founder of one of the country's first detective agencies, and Mary Todd Lincoln, who purchased a house on West Washington Boulevard in 1866. The John J. Glessners also lived on Washington until 1886, when they hired H. H. Richardson to design a house on Prairie Avenue. Music impresario Florenz Ziegfeld Jr. grew up on West Adams Street.

The west side's most famous and colorful resident was five-term Chicago mayor Carter Harrison. He purchased a house built in 1858 by Henry H. Honore, a southerner who made his fortune in real estate. Like Honore, whose daughter Bertha was to marry Potter Palmer and become the city's social doyenne, Harrison was a Kentuckian. Used to living on a vast expanse of land, he cantered around the neighborhood on his Kentucky thoroughbred. When Harrison purchased the property in 1866, it occupied an entire block on Ashland Avenue at Jackson Boulevard. To the east, toward Chicago's growing business district, was vacant prairie. Harrison's residence was a stately Italianate mansion, lovingly remembered by his son Carter Jr. (also a five-term mayor of Chicago) for its "breezy air of hospitality." It is remembered as the site where Mayor Harrison

was murdered in cold blood by a disgruntled candidate for public office. Although the house survived the great fire of 1871, as did most of the other grand houses on the near west side, it has been demolished. One by one, the prominent families moved and the mansions were replaced by factories, sweatshops, tenements, and railroad yards. The area west of Chicago's business district became infamous as the scene of the labor unrest that, in 1886, culminated in the Haymarket Riot. It also became famous as the port of entry for Chicago immigrants. In 1889, the mansion built in 1856 by Charles J. Hull was transformed into Hull-House, the world-renowned settlement house established by Jane Addams.

An area comparable in status to the west side developed on Chicago's near north side, across the Chicago River. William B. Ogden—who was among those who started the first successful railroad running west from Chicago—was elected mayor when the city incorporated in 1837. Shortly after, he built a large Greek Revival house on an entire block bounded by Ontario, Wabash (Cass), Erie, and Rush streets. Unlike the Clarke house, its south-side counterpart, Ogden's house was destroyed in the fire.

Many prominent Chicagoans preferred the near north side and created their own exclusive enclave in the area bounded by Michigan Avenue (Pine Street), Pearson Street, Dearborn Street, and Ohio Street. Realtors promoted the area, extolling its wide roadways, high ground, proximity to the lake, and location far from the stench of the stockyards. Steel magnate Joseph Ryerson lived there. So did Mayor Julian S. Rumsey, grain trader Abram Poole, dry-goods merchant John V. Farwell, and his brother Senator Charles Farwell. The Farwell houses, built side by side, both faced Chicago's quaint and picturesque stone Water

CHICAGO WATER TOWER AND WATERWORKS WITH HOUSES OF JOHN V. AND CHARLES FARWELL

Tower, which was completed in 1869 and survived the great Chicago fire.

Cyrus McCormick owned the north side's grandest house. McCormick, the inventor of the reaper, had a thriving farm-implements business that later merged into International Harvester. His brothers Leander and William both lived down the street. Cyrus Jr. and Leander's children all had houses in the neighborhood. So many McCormicks built their residences near the house of the family patriarch that the area became known as McCormickville.

The first generation of McCormicks no doubt wanted to live near the McCormick Reaper Works, which in 1848 was established just north of the Chicago River. Yet when the fire destroyed their factory in 1871 and the business relocated south of the river, the McCormicks and other residents did not abandon the neighborhood and instead rebuilt their houses almost immediately. By 1880, about 100 elegant mansions and townhouses had been constructed, but the area didn't retain its character long. The river historically was lined by factories, warehouses, and grain elevators, and as early as

GEORGE RUMSEY HOUSE, BEFORE AND AFTER THE GREAT FIRE OF 1871

the 1890s, commercial development pushed north. Hotels, office buildings, stores, and restaurants crowded out the single-family residences. Most of the grand houses have been torn down; some were converted into restaurants and offices, and one, the Nickerson mansion, has been reborn as a museum.

The great Chicago fire of 1871 produced utter devastation. It began on October 8 on Chicago's near west side in a cow barn belonging to the infamous Mrs. O'Leary. Chicago was a city built largely of wood, which was dry from days of drought, and fighting previous fires had left the city's fire department weary. Nothing but rain could stop the conflagration. By October 10, when the downpour finally came, almost every building in an area measuring three and a third square miles had been reduced to rubble. Three hundred lives and 30,000 buildings were lost. Ninety thousand people were homeless. The fire that could not be stopped jumped the Chicago River and

destroyed everything in its path up to Fullerton Avenue, which then marked Chicago's city limits.

The fire's impact was clearly conveyed in a letter written by a Chicago attorney to his mother in New Hampshire: "*We are in ruins*. All the business portion of the city has fallen prey to the fiery fiend. Our magnificent streets for acres & acres lined with elegant structures are a heap of sightless rubbish."

After the 1871 fire, many wealthy Chicagoans moved south and built palatial mansions along Prairie Avenue, only two miles south of downtown. The street's cachet developed when George Pullman and Marshall Field settled there. Prairie Avenue was a long street, but the grandest houses were located between 16th Street and 22nd. Other enclaves of prominent people—including Charles Hutchinson, the first president of the Art Institute of Chicago, and Marvin Hughitt, the president of the Chicago and North Western Railway—lived farther south

THE HOMES OF CHICAGO.—RESIDENCES OF PROMINENT CITIZENS ON PRAIRIE AVENUE.

Drawn by LOUIS BRAUNHOLD.

Engraved by J. M. WING & CO.

PRAIRIE AVENUE HOUSES

on Prairie and on the adjacent parallel side streets, Calumet, Indiana, and Michigan. Mrs. Arthur Meeker described the difference between the residents of the north and south ends of south Prairie Avenue to her children: "We ask them to our weddings but not to our dinner parties."

Endless superlatives were applied to Prairie Avenue. Mary Alice Molloy, in her essay on the street for *The Grand American Avenue*, quotes a variety of sources that refer to it as "the most looked up to street in the city," "the habitat of notably solvent citizens, "this golden spot," and "this nest of millionaires that was the hub of Chicago aristocracy and Americanism." Arthur

Meeker Jr. wrote a novel named *Prairie Avenue*, published in serial form in the *Chicago Tribune*, and he described that limited section of the avenue where he grew up as "the sunny street that held the sifted few." The famed political cartoonist John T. McCutcheon described the street, with perhaps a touch of overstatement, as "the holy of holies of the social life of the city." One comment noted that the wealth on the street "at last aroused the jealousy of New York."

A second enclave of successful Chicagoans developed south on Michigan Avenue, which from approximately 25th Street to 39th Street became known as Millionaire's Row. Meatpackers J. Ogden

MANSION REPLACED BY MIES VAN DER ROHE–DESIGNED APARTMENTS (1963), CORNER OF FULLERTON AND LAKEVIEW

Armour, Philip D. Armour, and John Cudahy lived there. Other well-known residents included brewer Conrad Seipp, department-store executive Emanuel Mandel, and stock speculator John "Bet a Million" Gates.

The time was "the Elegant Eighties." Social life was highly regimented, and the parties and travels of the wealthy were regularly reported in endless detail in the Chicago papers. Among the rich, a woman's life initially involved being her husband's companion, directing the family's social life, and managing staff, but as time went on, many women pursued their own activities vigorously, serving on boards and engaging in philan-

thropy. Chicago women formed literary societies, aided in the settlement movement, and donated time to promote the city's culture and welfare. For example, Chicago's undisputed society queen, Bertha Palmer, was also the chairperson of the Board of Lady Managers for the 1893 World's Columbian Exposition.

As early as the late 1880s, the south side began to lose its attraction. For years, residents of Prairie Avenue tolerated the dirt and noise of the railroad that ran just east of the street on a trestle over Lake Michigan. In 1861, the Illinois Central ran 16 trains on the route; during the 1880s, the railroad ran 60. Coal soot-blackened houses and train noise

WILLIAM RAINEY HARPER HOUSE (1894) IN HYDE PARK, WITH UNIVERSITY OF CHICAGO BUILDINGS BEYOND

rattled windows. The stockyards were only two miles away, close enough that when wind blew from the west, the smell became unbearable. By 1906, many owners of the south side's grand houses, including George Pullman, Philip D. Armour, and Marshall Field, had died. In 1885, when Potter and Bertha Palmer completed their new house several blocks north of the Water Tower on Lake Michigan, they inspired an exodus. Arthur Meeker Jr. recalls that when his family left Prairie Avenue in 1914, the move to the north side had become a stampede. With the growing popularity of the automobile, car dealers purchased the beautiful old houses on Michigan Avenue, demolished them, and built showrooms. Publishing houses and printing firms set up business in the Prairie Avenue mansions. Many once-grand residences became rooming houses. By the 1920s,

Prairie Avenue was cut off from the lake by a broad boulevard running south from Chicago's business district. Families like the Pullmans, who couldn't sell their parents' formerly glamorous homes and wanted to save on taxes, saw their mansions razed—leaving the streetscape full of gaping holes.

When Prairie Avenue no longer attracted Chicago millionaires, many prominent Chicagoans moved to Hyde Park and Kenwood. These two south-side neighborhoods, located next to each other, developed as railroad suburbs in the 1850s for families who wanted to live outside the city. In 1889, when Hyde Park and Kenwood were incorporated into Chicago, their streets were quiet and the houses were surrounded by broad lawns. When the University of Chicago opened in 1892 and Jackson Park (located in Hyde Park) was selected as the site of the 1893 World's Columbian Exposition, the formerly tranquil area gained worldwide recognition and became increasingly attractive as a place to live. Successful businessmen, including lumber merchant Martin Ryerson, meatpacker Gustavus Swift, and clothier Joseph Schaffner, built large houses in a variety of styles. Some houses, like those of Julius Rosenwald or Edward Morris, could be mistaken for country estates in Lake Forest. John Graves Shedd, the president of Marshall Field & Company, built an imposing château on Drexel, one of Chicago's grand boulevards. Frederick Robie, a bicycle manufacturer, hired Frank Lloyd Wright to fashion a spectacularly different house facing what was, in 1909, open prairie. Although some fine residences have been lost, Hyde Park and Kenwood remain attractive, cohesive communities with streetscapes resembling those in the North Shore suburbs of Evanston and Wilmette.

By 1893, when the World's Fair opened, the area known to all of Chicago as the Gold Coast was the premier place to live. Although Lake Shore Drive between Oak Street and North Avenue had opened in 1875, it was then regarded more as a fashionable destination for Sunday outings than as a place to build elegant mansions. Development adjacent to Lake Shore Drive occurred a decade later, but when it happened, the effect was enormous. The parade north that began when Potter Palmer built his castle there in the mid-1880s drew people out of the previously fashionable areas on Chicago's west, south, and near north sides. Family after family abandoned their houses to establish new ones in the area bounded by Lake Shore Drive, Lincoln Park, North Dearborn Parkway, and Oak Street. After developing State Street, the Chicago Loop's most popular shopping area, Palmer had embarked on

creating the city's most desirable residential locale. While building his own residence, he began construction of houses on the surrounding vacant land to sell or rent to his friends. His endeavor was a great success and, to quote Meeker, whole colonies of "castellinos" sprang up.

While the Palmer mansion was under construction, a stately Queen Anne–style residence was being built for Chicago's first archbishop on land the Catholic Church had owned since 1843. As Palmer sold off property to amass personal wealth, the archdiocese subdivided its surrounding land and sold lots to fund the good works of the Church.

A string of 34 stone mansions rivaling those on Prairie Avenue was constructed along Lake Shore Drive. Residents included attorney Robert Todd Lincoln, grocery tycoon Franklin MacVeagh, and mimeograph-machine magnate A. B. Dick. Immediately west and parallel to Lake Shore Drive was a street named to honor John Jacob Astor, the founder of the American Fur Company. His fur traders had operated in the Chicago area during the early 19th century, so the name had a historical connotation. But the greater attraction for prospective residents was the association with Astor as New York's wealthiest business tycoon. The blocks immediately west of Lake Shore Drive had fewer freestanding houses. New construction on Astor Street was denser and generally consisted of townhouses with common walls on 25-foot lots. Chicago's population had doubled from 500,000 in 1880 to over 1 million residents by 1890, and houses built on narrow sites could accommodate a considerable number of affluent Chicagoans. North State and Dearborn Parkway townhouses repeated the development pattern of Astor. Architects from the East Coast, such as McKim, Mead & White, joined the ranks of prestigious Chicago architects including Burnham &

POTTER PALMER MANSION (1884), WITH MACVEAGH HOUSE (1887) TO THE NORTH ON LAKE SHORE DRIVE

Root, Holabird & Roche, Howard Van Doren Shaw, and David Adler to create elegant Gold Coast residences.

Some families, such as the senior Arthur Meekers and brewer Francis Dewes, built houses north of the Lake Shore Drive area between Oak Street and North Avenue. Although a large concentration of mansions like those found on the Gold Coast never developed adjacent to Lincoln Park, the area had great appeal. David Adler designed a row of townhouses on Lakeview facing the park that are reminiscent of those in London's Kensington. Some of the large houses in the neighborhood remain standing, but many have been replaced by apartment buildings. The mansion of Andrew E. Leicht, who made a for-

tune in the brewing and lumber industries, stood at the corner of Fullerton and Lakeview. In 1963, it was replaced by an apartment building, the last steel-and-glass high-rise Mies van der Rohe designed in Chicago.

After the turn of the 20th century, few single-family houses were built on Chicago's Gold Coast or facing Lincoln Park. In 1914, William O. Goodman, who had a beautiful 1880s house in Kenwood, hired Howard Van Doren Shaw to fashion a stunning residence known as the Court of the Golden Hand, on Astor Street. David Adler designed his most elegant townhouse there in 1921 for Joseph Ryerson Jr. In 1928, Holabird and Root designed a chic Art Deco residence north on Astor for Edward P. Russell. Characterized by a simplicity of form, it was totally unlike its historically inspired neighbors. These houses of the teens and twenties were the exceptions, and the completion of the Russell House marked the end of an era. Houses were torn down and replaced by apartment buildings at every opportunity. As cars became more prevalent and rail transportation to outlying Chicago suburbs became easier, many of Chicago's leading families moved into luxury apartments for the winter social season and spent summers in their country houses on the North Shore. Some spent parts of the winter in Montecito or Palm Beach.

After 1905, when architect Benjamin Marshall designed the Georgian Revival Marshall Apartments—Lake Shore Drive's first apartment building—the Gold Coast took on a new appearance. During the 1910s and 1920s, many of the stately mansions facing Lake Michigan were demolished and replaced by luxury multifamily buildings with apartment interiors that rivaled the grand spaces of Lake Forest mansions. This trend continued on Lake Shore Drive through the 1960s, although the modern high-rises that replaced them were expensive but architecturally mundane. The Marshall has been replaced by a larger building. Only eight houses now remain on Lake Shore Drive. These include elegant city residences designed by McKim, Mead & White and Benjamin Marshall. The smaller townhouses along Astor Street and State and Dearborn parkways are now punctuated by high-rises, but many of these houses are being lovingly restored.

What remains today of Chicago's other great houses? Many of those in areas such as Hyde Park, Kenwood, and the Gold Coast still stand; these dense neighborhoods of elegant residences are highly prized and have been designated historic districts. The mansions in areas such as the west side and McCormickville have all but disap-

EDWARD P. RUSSELL RESIDENCE, 1928–29

peared. Cyrus McCormick's mansion is long gone. A section of Leander McCormick's house peeks from behind a restaurant. A shop building containing a store occupies the site of the houses Charles and John V. Farwell built facing Chicago's Water Tower.

INTRODUCTION

POTTER PALMER MANSION, WITH APARTMENT BUILDING TO THE NORTH ON LAKE SHORE DRIVE

Chicago is a dynamic city. Hard-working businessmen built its great houses. Entrepreneurial developers have guided—and not always for the best—Chicago's transformation from a city of single-family residences to one that also embraces apartment living. Today, considerable effort focuses on preserving Chicago's residential masterpieces. It is a battle fought with the same aggressive spirit that has guided the city's growth since 1871.

—Susan Benjamin

GREAT HOUSES: STYLE AND THEORY

FASHION AND SOCIAL POSITION were factors that shaped the houses of prominent Chicagoans. It is easy to argue that design and style often said more about homeowners' wealth, taste, and status than did the size of their houses. But Chicagoans did not build houses of the scale and opulence of their New York counterparts, even though the fortunes amassed by Chicago's meat-packers, brewers, dry-goods merchants, steel moguls, and inventors would have allowed them to. Perhaps at the end of the 19th century Chicago was still perceived to some extent as the frontier, a place where people went to make their fortunes rather than display their wealth. If Chicago was perceived as a great American city after the attention drawn to it by the 1893 World's Fair, New York was perceived by its residents as a great world city. When Chicagoans chose to display wealth, they competed with one another rather than with New Yorkers, although New York architects such as Richard Morris Hunt; McKim, Mead & White; and Charles Platt received commissions to build houses in Chicago for Marshall Field and William Borden, Bryan Lathrop, Robert Patterson, Edward T. Blair, and Arthur Meeker Sr. Wealthy New York families measured their houses against the châteaux and villas of Europe and the large, opulent city houses of London and Paris. Although wealthy Chicagoans also traveled to Europe, for most, their experiences didn't translate into a desire to build houses on a larger scale.

Chicago houses did reflect the growing ease of travel. The East Coast could be reached by an overnight train ride, and the time required for a transatlantic crossing kept diminishing as new, faster, and bigger ocean liners came into service. Exposed to other cultures, wealthy Chicagoans began collecting art, decorative arts, books, and even looking to America's West for Native American artifacts. These diverse collections, including paintings, sculpture, armor, weapons, fossils, mummies, gemstones, and meteorites, formed the initial holdings of institutions such as the Art Institute, the Field Museum, and the Newberry Library. They also required houses with rooms designed to display them. Sometimes these spaces took on specific themes: French rooms, Tudor rooms, and more exotically decorated Moorish, Egyptian, Pompeian, or Chinese rooms. Today, images of these spaces are hard for us to look at, as they suggest overdecorated stage sets, lacking the continuity and consistency of architectural style and detail to which we are accustomed. Yet architects responded to their clients' desire to display acquisitions as well as wealth, helping fuel the eclecticism of the time and the fashion for floor plans composed of distinctly different rooms, each decorated to reflect a different theme based on its use, furnishings, or displayed artwork.

Chicago differed from New York not only in the size and opulence of houses built but in architectural tastes. Late 19th- and early 20th-century

"ROMANESQUE" LAKE SHORE DRIVE LOOKING NORTH FROM SCHILLER STREET
SHOWING MACVEAGH, BARRETT, AND OGDEN AND BARBARA ARMOUR HOUSES

Chicago architecture is renowned for the development of the skyscraper and, in residential architecture, of the Prairie School. The former put forward the expression of frame construction as a new aesthetic and the latter, the development of new ideas about interior space and its visual connection to the outside. Both became cornerstones for the development of 20th-century modern architecture. Yet these two progressive approaches seem to have little to do with the history of the great city houses built in Chicago between the 1870s and the 1920s, as these were designed in traditional architectural styles based on historical forms and details. If the

progressive mindset of architects in Chicago and their clients' foresight created the milieu that produced important architectural inventions, how does this relate to the historically eclectic houses that were being built? This presumed disconnect would explain why many extraordinary houses have been neglected by 20th-century historians. It has been argued that the "Chicago frame" was an economic and pragmatic invention, not an intellectual breakthrough, as described by European architectural historians. It has also been suggested that the spatial ideas of the Prairie School were an extension of Arts and Crafts architecture awaiting only the

European addition of geometric abstraction. However, it is possible that, seen from a slightly different perspective, many of the houses that fill this book can be understood as both progressive for their time and inventive within the context that defines them.

In the 1870s and early 1880s in Chicago, urban houses were predominantly French-influenced. These houses—loosely described as châteauesque, Second Empire in style—were characterized by mansard roofs, projecting bays that were usually flat rather than angled, and ubiquitous corner towers, even when a house wasn't built on a corner lot. The architectural profession and American architectural education were all influenced by the methods of the French academy, even though at that time few American students had attended the Ecole des Beaux-Arts in Paris. New York architect Richard Morris Hunt was the first American to graduate from the Ecole, returning to the United States in 1855. For years to come, Hunt, often referred to as the "dean of American architecture," championed the construction of buildings based on French design.

The great fire of 1871 had a significant impact on the look of Chicago's residential architecture. Thereafter, houses within the city limits were required to be of fireproof construction. Expensive houses were built of stone, banishing wood houses in the Victorian-era Queen Anne style and its shingled derivatives, to the suburbs. Although brick and stone Tudor houses and brick Georgians competed with limestone-clad French-style houses, the Romanesque Revival, popularized by another Ecole des Beaux-Arts graduate, H. H. Richardson, transformed the look of Chicago's city houses.

In 1924, Chicago architect Louis Sullivan believed that the classicism of the Chicago 1893 World's Fair would set back the cause of architec-

ture 50 years. Its influence was certainly great. The Chicago fair gave us America's City Beautiful movement. The adaptation of classicism by large architectural firms such as D. H. Burnham & Company in Chicago; McKim, Mead & White in New York; and Richardson's successor firm, Shepley, Rutan, & Coolidge, in Boston, produced some of the most enduring civic and institutional buildings of the 20th century. The appeal of rules-based architecture, as taught in the Beaux-Arts curriculums of American schools of architecture, is easy to understand. Its suitability for urban building ensembles had already been demonstrated by the Court of Honor at the Chicago World's Fair. However, in Chicago, unlike in New York, classicism was largely the domain of civic buildings and had only a limited impact on the city's residential buildings. The practitioners of classicism then building houses in Chicago were largely out-of-town architects such as McKim, Mead & White; Shepley, Rutan & Coolidge; and Charles Platt. The older generation of Chicago architects, such as P. B. Wight or Solon Beman, almost never embraced classicism, perhaps because only a few of them were offered the opportunity to build at the 1893 Chicago World's Fair. One exception was Francis Whitehouse, who designed a number of classical houses in the 1890s. The younger generation of eclectic architects, such as Howard Van Doren Shaw, James Gamble Rogers, and David Adler, frequently built classical houses after 1910.

In 1891, the well-known American architectural critic Montgomery Schuyler commented on the preponderance of Romanesque-style houses being built in the city: "Another characteristic of the domestic architecture of Chicago . . . is the evidence it affords of an admiration for the work of Mr. Richardson." Schuyler decried these houses, stretching on for street after street, as "undiscriminating" imitations of Henry Hobson Richardson's work. Arguably the greatest 19th-century American architect, Richardson popularized the Romanesque Revival to the extent that the style became known as "Richardsonian Romanesque." Despite its medieval European origins, it was lauded by critics and accepted by architects as the first original American architectural style.

Why was the Romanesque seen as uniquely suited to American buildings? Why did it persist in Chicago long after it fell out of fashion elsewhere? What aspects of Richardson's architecture set it apart from the work of his contemporaries, and why did it influence Chicago's residential and civic architecture so strongly?

Romanesque architecture was highly picturesque in the arrangement of its parts, providing flexibility in internal planning. This allowed the functional relationships required by late 19th-century civic, institutional, and large residential buildings to be addressed. It was an architecture that appeared assembled from primary geometric volumes: cubes, cylinders, and cones. Its stylistic elements were columns, walls, and arches, and this trait gave it both simplicity and the appearance of structural honesty, which many American architects were striving for in their work. In short, in the 1880s and 1890s the style was modern, and it differed markedly from the eclectic styles that preceded it.

Richardson's genius went beyond being the first to recognize and realize the potential in Romanesque architecture. At its most primary level, architecture is made of structure and of space created by enclosing surfaces, but architects frequently isolate rather than integrate these elements. Richardson's architecture brilliantly combined the handling of flat surfaces and volumes. Richardson conceived of walls not just as thin surfaces stretched around interior spaces but as having thickness, capable of containing space within them. To create this perception, he exposed the front and back surfaces of his walls at entryways and balconies, giving his buildings an even greater sense of massiveness. This may be seen in his designs for Chicago houses for J. J. Glessner and Franklin MacVeagh. These characteristics, combined with Richardson's unmatched ability to simplify the forms of his buildings, made his architecture the dominant influence on two generations of American architects.

In Chicago, it was John Wellborn Root who, even more than Louis Sullivan, understood the lessons of Richardson's architecture. Like Richardson, Root, who was Daniel Burnham's partner, died in his 40s, cutting short a brilliant career. Root was the designer of unprecedented commercial buildings, such as the Monadnock Block (1891) in Chicago. Sullivan's most important civic buildings, such as the Auditorium Building (1886–89) and his later bank buildings, are all indebted to Richardson's Romanesque. In his tall buildings, such as the Wainwright Building in St. Louis, Sullivan often struggled against the modernity of the Chicago School, choosing to suppress the horizontality of the steel frame in favor of expressing the building's loftiness. Sullivan's greatest contribution was to take the vocabulary of Romanesque ornament, leaves and berries, systematize its design, and then apply it at different scales throughout his buildings as a unifying element. From this example, Frank Lloyd Wright developed the idea that all the elements of a building, from its plan to its leaded-glass windows, might derive from the same compositional motif. Sullivan's ideas about the relationship between a building's form and its function, as well as his appreciation of Richardson's work in Chicago, are found in his "Kindergarten Chats," first published in 52 installments in the *Interstate Architect and Builder* between 1901 and 1902. In one of the chats, called "Oasis," he wrote in praise of Richardson and his Marshall Field Wholesale store (1887) in Chicago, "Let us pause, my son, at this oasis in our desert . . . Four-square and brown it stands in physical fact, a monument to trade . . . impressed with the stamp of large and forceful personality: artistically it stands as the oration of one who knows well how to choose his words . . . the outpouring of a copious, direct, large and simple mind." In his theoretical writing, Sullivan—as Wright later did—described what became known as "organic theory." The word *organic* suggested the process by which all the parts of a building were interrelated, as if they had grown from the same living organism. It is less known that John Root, influenced by the writings of English architects such as Augustus Pugin and William Morris, was writing and teaching the same things in Chicago in the 1880s and 1890s. In *John Wellborn Root: The Meanings of Architecture*, edited by Donald Hoffmann, Root's architectural philosophy is made clear. Root wrote, "Styles grow by the careful study of all the conditions which lie about each architectural problem . . . broad influences of climate, of national habits and institutions will in time create the type, and this is the only style worth considering." About the use of precedent, he opined, "It means rather to use all that men have done, to use it all intelligently and consistently . . . and to make sure that the particular thing chosen for the given purpose shall in short grow out of it." Predating Frank Lloyd Wright and Le Corbusier's pronouncements from the 1920s, in the 1880s Root wrote that "the interior plan of the house is its vital part, from which everything else grows" and "any new design should be carefully

adjusted to its neighbors." Finally, with respect to Root's own design sensibilities, Richardson's importance as a simplifier of architectural form, and the abstraction that would later characterize 20th-century architecture, he wrote, "The value of plain surfaces in every building is not to be over-estimated. Strive for them, and when the fates place at your disposal a good, generous sweep of masonry, accept it frankly and thank God." For *Scribner's* magazine he wrote, "Richardson's influence has always tended to make architecture more simple and direct, and it has led architects more generally to avoid the hideous mass of shams which in America preceded him."

In assessing the desire to create an original, modern, and uniquely American architecture, we forget the mindset and intellectual frame of reference within which late 19th-century architects worked. Lawrence Weaver, early 20th century English architectural critic and biographer of architect Edwin Lutyens, explained the 19th century's idea of the relationship of eclecticism to invention when he wrote, "Originality lies in the infinite arrangement of traditional architectural form regardless of provenance." Although Gothic Revival, Victorian, and Queen Anne architecture were picturesque in their arrangement of volumes, all providing for a modern flexibility in the internal planning of buildings, they were all overtly based on European historical motifs. Except for Gothic architecture, they were rarely expressive of the building's structure or construction. Yet we can apply a 20th-century definition of modernism in architecture to the Romanesque and the Romanesque Revival, which are characterized by the expression of structure, the simplification of forms and surfaces, the near elimination of ornament, and the arrangement of a building's internal spaces in relation to its function. These theoretical ideas, expressed in Chicago by Root and Sullivan, were intellectually linked to the Romanesque Revival. This relationship explains both its popularity and its persistence in Chicago residential design as an expression of Americanness and progressive thought. In light of this, and the buildings he con-tinued to design, perhaps Louis Sullivan's famous comment about the impact of the 1893 World's Fair really referred to the further development of American Romanesque, not the Chicago School or the Prairie School of architecture as 20th century historians assumed.

—Stuart Cohen

GREAT HOUSES OF
CHICAGO

1871–1921

ULMENHEIM

Eliphalet Wickes Blatchford House

375 LaSalle Street

Peter Bonnett Wight, Drake & Wight, 1874–76

ELEVATION DRAWING

VIEW FROM LA SALLE STREET

Many of Chicago's greatest houses were built for men who gained prominence primarily as successful businessmen. However, Eliphalet W. Blatchford was better known for his extensive philanthropy. He was an important bibliophile, a devoted public servant, and an ardent supporter of the missionary work of the Congregationalist Church.

Eliphalet Blatchford, named for his grandfather Eliphalet Wickes (1769–1850), was born in 1826 in Stillwater, New York, but moved to Chicago as a young boy when his father became pastor of the city's First Presbyterian Church. Shortly after his graduation from Illinois College in Jacksonville, Illinois, he moved to St. Louis, Missouri, to work in the lead and oil industries. After returning to Chicago in 1854 to manage his company's local office, he established E. W. Blatchford & Company. His firm was primarily known as a plumbing-supply house, but it also manufactured lead shot and other metal products. He eventually turned his company over to his sons and focused instead on his philanthropic work.

Blatchford's tremendous business success was played down in his 1914 obituary, in which he was praised for his leadership in education and for helping to establish two important Chicago

STAIR HALL

MUSIC ROOM WITH ORGAN

libraries, the Newberry and the Crerar. Walter Loomis Newberry (1804–1868), a successful Chicago banker and businessman, willed half of his estate for the establishment of a free library. Blatchford served as one of two estate trustees charged with creating the Newberry Library. He became president of its board, a position he held for 29 years. Established in 1887 and built in 1892, the Newberry continues to serve as a reference library for the study of history and the humanities and contains the papers of many important Chicagoans, including Blatchford. In 1891 the will of John Crerar made Blatchford trustee for his $3 million estate, which in 1894 established the Crerar Library, emphasizing technology and the natural sciences.

A half dozen years after he began working, Blatchford joined in the Civil War effort, serving as an active member and treasurer of the U.S. Sanitary Commission. For more than 30 years, he was the president of the Chicago Theological Seminary, an institution that later became affiliated with the University of Chicago. In addition, he was a founder of the Chicago Manual Training

DINING ROOM SHOWING TABLE AND CHAIRS DESIGNED BY P. B. WIGHT

School, the Chicago City Missionary Society, the Chicago Congregational Club, the New West Educational Commission, and the Bohemian Mission of Chicago, which started in his home.

His wife, Mary Blatchford, gained recognition in her own right. Under her auspices, a very early kindergarten in Chicago, possibly the first, was started at the Blatchford residence in the 1870s. Their own children and their neighbors attended the school, which grew to accommodate more than three dozen students. There, Mrs. Blatchford introduced the scheme of kindergarten teaching

laid out by German educator Friedrich Froebel and was active in introducing the methods into Chicago's public schools. For 25 years, she served as the president of the Chicago Froebel Kindergarten Association. This approach became well known because Chicago's preeminent Prairie School architect, Frank Lloyd Wright, received Froebel kindergarten training and credited it with influencing his work.

Originally, the Blatchfords lived in a wood clapboard Second Empire-style house that was built in 1862—it was handsome but hardly

ELIPHALET BLATCHFORD IN HIS LIBRARY

extraordinary. After the house burned in Chicago's 1871 fire, they engaged Peter Bonnett Wight to design a much more substantial and elaborate house to occupy the same site. That house *was* extraordinary. Like their first house, it was to be called Ulmenheim, meaning "home under the elms." Sarah B. Landau, in her 1981 study of Wight's work, looked carefully at the Blatchford residence, noting its French influences. Like many of its contemporaries, the house was topped by a mansard roof; French architecture had not lost its cachet. Yet the design was highly

original with predominantly Gothic Revival detailing. Landau pointed out the appropriateness of the Gothic associations, as they reflected Blatchford's devotion to God and commitment to traditional Christian values.

On the exterior, slate roofs, windows topped by pointed arches, massive brick chimneys, red sandstone and brickwork in a variety of patterns, and gray granite columns all combined to form rich textures. The richness was equally compelling in the house's interior decor. As Landau mentioned, figured papers and borders with stylized patterns

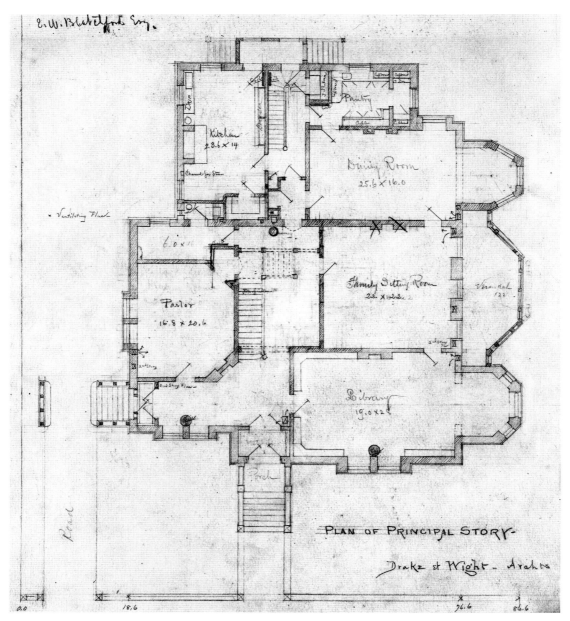

FIRST FLOOR PLAN

covered the walls and ceilings. Furnishings—settees, chairs, bookcases, ornate Eastlake-style fireplaces—were all designed and placed by the architect to fit into their settings. The dense patterns found throughout the walls, rugs, and furniture of the library work with the room's paintings, books, and general clutter to create a warm, comfortable atmosphere where Blatchford could indulge a favorite pastime, reading. Bookcases were inscribed with inspirational mottoes—for example, "Footprints on the Sands of Time" referred to a case of history books. Blatchford's personal library contained more than 5,000 volumes, and with books by John Ruskin, Daniel Webster, Washington Irving, and Charles Dickens, was one of the finest in Chicago.

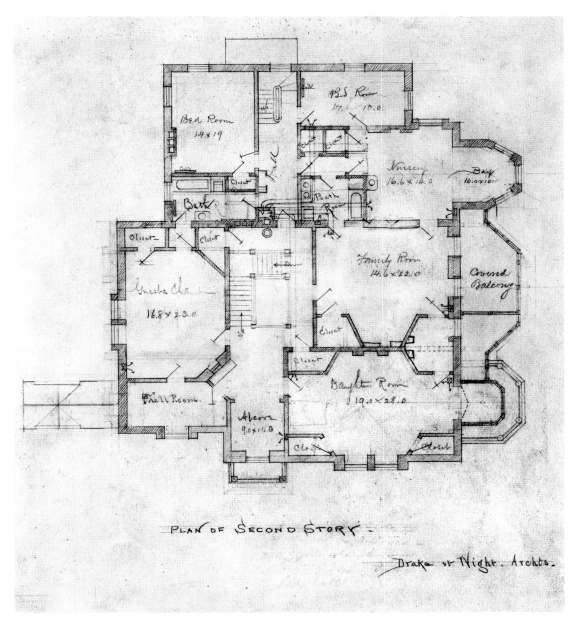

SECOND FLOOR PLAN

The Blatchford house, a place where Chicago's civic and religious leaders met to shape the city's social history, was demolished in 1929. When it was taken down, a public ceremony was held to open the cornerstone that had been sealed since it was laid in 1876. Family members, friends, and interested spectators, including the Blatchford's coachman, gathered to watch as personal mementos—a small Bible, a sermon preached by Blatchford's father in 1855, a set of family photographs, and a friend's calling card—were uncovered. The event marked the poignant end to an era.

MARSHALL FIELD HOUSE

1905 South Prairie Avenue

Richard Morris Hunt, 1875

VIEW FROM PRAIRIE AVENUE

VIEW FROM THE SOUTH

Marshall Field was Chicago's counterpart to New York's multimillionaire William K. Vanderbilt. At the time of his death in 1906, Field's estate is said to have been valued at $100 million, one of the largest private fortunes in the United States. Today no family name other than Wrigley has equal recognition in Chicago. Field, called Chicago's merchant prince, founded the city's most fashionable department store, Marshall Field & Company, and bequeathed $8 million to establish the Field Museum of Natural History, an icon on Chicago's lakefront.

In the early 1870s, when they sought an architect, the Fields turned to Richard Morris Hunt, who was introducing French architecture to America and becoming New York's most prominent architect. By the mid-1890s, when Hunt designed Biltmore in Asheville, North Carolina, for George W. Vanderbilt, he was established as the preeminent architect of the Gilded Age. When Field engaged him, Hunt had begun designing opulent houses for New York's robber barons. But for his Prairie Avenue residence, Field was attracted to Hunt because of the architect's New England pedigree, not his growing reputation as a society architect. Field wanted a no-frills house that conveyed an image of dignity and simplicity—at least on the exterior.

Field's château on Prairie Avenue had a stately presence. It was deep-red brick with incised

MAIN HALL LOOKING TOWARD STAIRCASE

limestone trim and was topped by a steep slate mansard roof. Its floor plan, with a central hall-way flanked by symmetrical rooms that had their centers on axis, clearly came from Hunt's Ecole des Beaux-Arts training. He ingeniously oriented the house to the south, connecting the diagonally-oriented dining room and library with a semicir-cular conservatory. During this period, incorporat-ing a conservatory within the plan of the house became prevalent in grand dwellings.

The spartan exterior of the Field house gave no hint of its lavish interior, which was designed by L. Marcotte, of New York and Paris, a firm that also did the Cyrus McCormick house and many Vanderbilt interiors. The Field residence's reputed $2 million cost was reflected in its etched-glass front doors, curving walnut staircase, ornate carved woodwork, marble trim, and elabo-rate sterling-silver doorknobs and key plates.

Moneyed Chicagoans, including the Fields, regularly entertained in lavish style, but no event rivaled the Fields' January 1886 Mikado Ball, one of the grandest social occasions in Chicago his-tory. The ball honored 17-year-old Marshall II and 14-year-old Ethel, the two Field children. More than 500 guests of all ages were invited. Gilbert and Sullivan's operetta *The Mikado*, at the time the most popular stage success in

LIBRARY

America, provided the party theme. Parents and children, all dressed in exotic colorful costumes, arrived in fancy carriages drawn by teams of horses. Prairie Avenue was aglow, illuminated by special calcium lights. No Chicago caterer was felt to be adequate, so Sherry's of New York was engaged to supply the food, linen, and silver, which arrived in private railroad cars. Decorators transformed the house into a Japanese village. On one side of the hall was a miniature pagoda, where Chicago society's favorite bandleader, Johnny Hand, conducted. Doors were taken out and replaced with fringed curtains of beaded wood, ivory, and glass as would have been found

in the houses of wealthy Japanese. All of the walls were covered with satin and bamboo screens, and lanterns and parasols hung from the ceiling. James McNeill Whistler designed two of the party favors each guest took home. The cost of the ball exceeded $75,000, a hefty sum in 1886.

Marshall Field came from a modest background, but, like many of his contemporaries who migrated to Chicago, he was highly ambitious. He was born in 1834 on a farm outside Conway, Massachusetts. At the age of 18 he became a clerk in a dry-goods store in Pittsfield, but he left for Chicago in 1856 to work for a larger merchandising concern and soon became a junior partner.

Office Copy
M. FIELD.

Nº 8

SOUTH ELEVATION

By 1865, he organized the firm of Field, Palmer & Leiter. After Potter Palmer left to pursue his highly successful real-estate ventures and Levi Leiter retired, Field established Marshall Field & Company in 1881. Following the credo "Right or wrong, the customer is always right," Field pioneered in customer service. The store carried high-quality merchandise, instituted citywide deliveries, had a liberal return policy, and featured artistic window displays. It functioned as a fashionable social center with popular dining rooms, a theater ticket office, and everything to "give the lady what she wants." The store carried Marshall Field's name for more than 100 years until, despite the protests of many Chicagoans, it became Macy's in 2006.

Field's wife Nannie Douglas Scott died in 1896. In 1904, he remarried the widowed socialite Mrs. Arthur Delia Caton. Field died two years later, at age 71. Mrs. Field inherited the house but lived there only until shortly before World War I, when she moved to Washington, D.C.—leaving the residence in the hands of a housekeeper and caretaker. Before she died in 1937, Delia Caton Field deeded the house to Marshall Field III, who gave it to the American Association of Arts and Industries, stipulating that the structure be used as an industrial arts school. Called the New Bauhaus, the school was run by László Moholy-Nagy, who had taught at the German Bauhaus. The house was remodeled to accommodate the modernist aesthetic, but after only two years the New Bauhaus closed. In 1944, the school became the Institute of Design, and in 1949, it merged with the Illinois Institute of Technology. The house was left empty and, like most of the mansions on Prairie Avenue, was demolished.

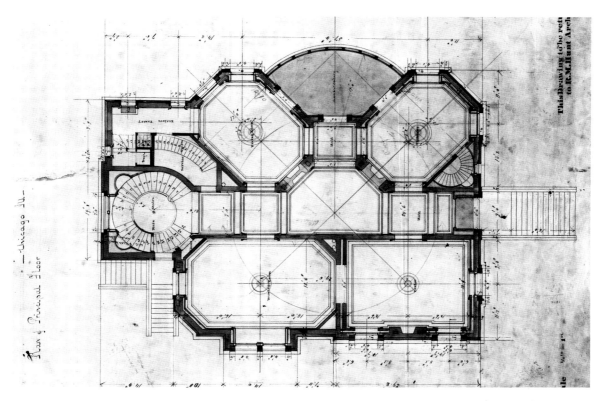

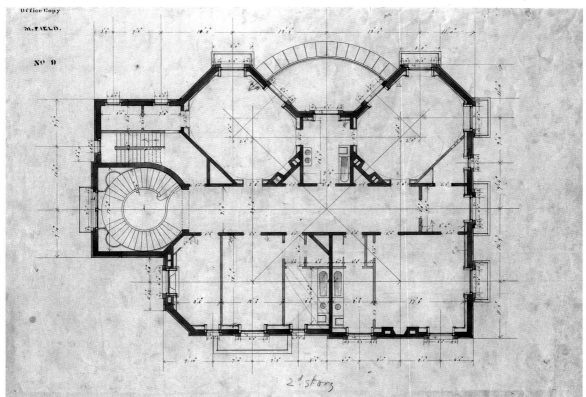

FIRST AND SECOND FLOOR PLANS

CYRUS HALL McCORMICK HOUSE

675 Rush Street

Cudell & Blumenthal, 1875–79

VIEW FROM RUSH STREET

VIEW FROM ERIE STREET

Cyrus Hall McCormick invented the first commercially successful reaper. His invention, and his ability to mass-produce and market it on a vast scale, revolutionized agriculture and helped transform the United States economy from agrarian to industrial. McCormick founded a huge farm-implement company that became International Harvester, making him one of Chicago's leading industrialists.

Work consumed McCormick's time and not until he was 70 years old did he build a house commensurate with his business success. His residence took four years to finish and was one of the most lavish in Chicago. Recalling Napoleon III's then-recent additions to the Louvre, it featured steep mansard roofs topped by elaborate cresting, rusticated stone walls, oeil-de-boeuf windows, a bold central tower, and richly ornamented window surrounds. The house occupied an entire block on Chicago's near north side in an area where so many members of the McCormick family built houses it was called McCormickville.

Cyrus McCormick's house was comparable in size and lavishness to George Pullman and Marshall Field's extravagant residences on fashionable Prairie Avenue. Its first floor was distinguished by tall decorated ceilings, elegant wood paneling, exotic wallpapers, and overstuffed furnishings laid out to create

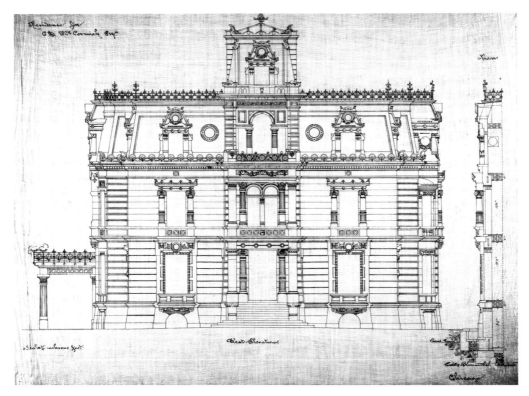

WEST ELEVATION

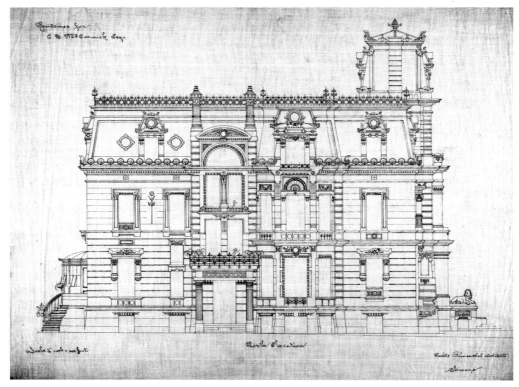

NORTH ELEVATION

GARDEN

proper arrangements, not opportunities for conversation. The artwork consisted of reproductions of Renaissance paintings and sculpture.

Cyrus McCormick was born in 1809 on a 532-acre farm known as Walnut Grove, in Rockbridge County, Virginia. For two decades his prosperous father, Robert, experimented with the design of a mechanical horse-drawn harvester to replace the hand-held scythe, the instrument that had been used to harvest grain for thousands of years. The elder McCormick gave up in frustration and turned over the project to his 22-year-old son. Cyrus had no formal education but displayed a talent for invention. After making several refinements to his father's design, he demonstrated the reaper in 1831 at Steeles Tavern, Virginia, and patented it in 1834. McCormick had heard that a man named Obed Hussey had invented a reaper, and he wanted to

create a superior machine that would dominate the market.

The reaper, which Cyrus was manufacturing and selling from the blacksmith shop at his family farm, wasn't an immediate success. Observers agreed that the machine could do the work of several men, but farmers were afraid it was too complicated to handle. In addition, money was scarce and labor was plentiful. In the mid-1840s, McCormick began to manufacture machines in Cincinnati and in Brockport, New York. He soon realized that to be successful, he had to develop creative marketing strategies and relocate his operation.

McCormick's largest market was in the midwestern grain-growing states, where land was flat, farms were cheap, and labor was scarce. He needed to be in the distribution center of the country. In 1847, Cyrus moved to Chicago, the heart of the Midwest, and built a large plant.

HALL

To raise the necessary capital to begin mass production, McCormick formed a partnership with William B. Ogden, the mayor and one of Chicago's leading citizens. After buying Ogden out in 1849, he developed the strategy that was to ensure success. He sold the machine for the cost of a down payment on it. The rest of the price was due if the reaper lived up to its guaranteed performance. Unafraid of competition, he blanketed the newspapers with advertisements carrying testimonials. McCormick worked hard to retain the loyalty of his sales agents and the interest of his farming clientele. In 1851, the reaper won the first of many awards when it took the gold medal at London's Crystal Palace Exhibition, an honor that put the invention on the map and made its inventor a celebrity. By 1856, his company's production reached 4,000 reapers a year and McCormick was becoming a millionaire. When Cyrus McCormick died, in 1884, the McCormick Harvesting Machine Company was producing 40,000 machines a year and had a worldwide market.

The company Cyrus started was a family venture. His younger brother, Leander, supervised the factory, and his brother William handled accounting and purchasing. When family infighting led to Leander's departure in 1880, Cyrus McCormick groomed his son Cyrus Jr. to run the company. He was one of five children born to Cyrus and his wife Nettie Fowler McCormick, a 26-year-old schoolteacher Cyrus Sr. had married

STAIR HALL

STUDY

in 1858. Cyrus Jr. took over as president of the McCormick firm upon his father's death in 1884. In 1902, it merged with four smaller farm-implement companies to form the International Harvester Company.

The McCormicks held their first party in the Rush Street house in 1880 to celebrate Cyrus Jr.'s 21st birthday. The *Chicago Tribune* described the event as a "soiree musicale" at the McCormicks'

"new palatial residence," with 300 "distinguished" attendees. The house's interior was praised for "so much that is beautiful and artistic." The residence, which had a third-floor ballroom and a concert hall, was run by a staff of 12.

Cyrus McCormick lived in his new house for only four years. Although his wife Nettie later had a country estate in Lake Forest, she continued to spend time at her 45-room city place until her

LIVING ROOM

LIBRARY

DINING ROOM

death in 1923 at age 88. Her son Harold lived in the mansion following his divorce from Edith Rockefeller McCormick. The coach house at the rear was transformed into a library in order to house archives containing more than a million manuscript items pertaining to the McCormicks.

In 1945, the stately residence of Cyrus Hall McCormick was sold for $450,000 and demolished. The excellent archival material that had been gathered was donated to the State Historical Society of Wisconsin.

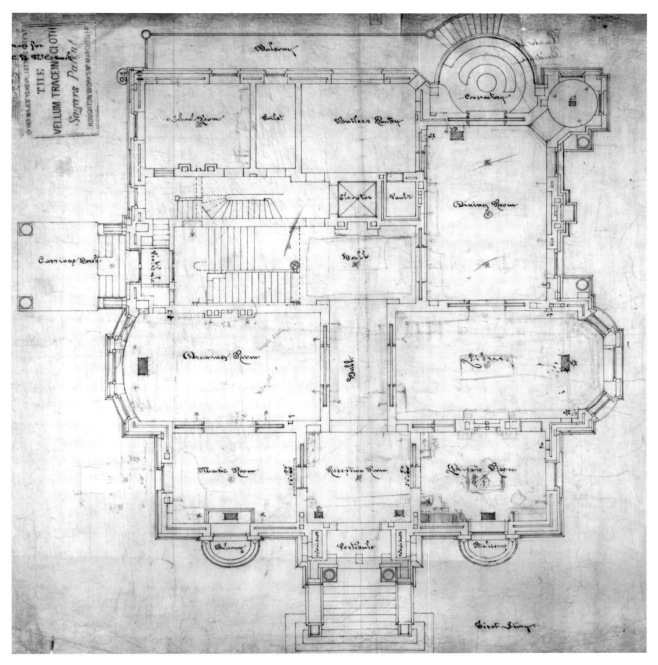

FIRST FLOOR PLAN

GEORGE M. PULLMAN HOUSE

1729 South Prairie Avenue

Henry S. Jaffray; Solon S. Beman

1876, 1891, 1896

VIEW FROM PRAIRIE AVENUE

VIEW FROM THE SOUTH

Opulent, lavish, ostentatious, flamboyant are all words that come to mind when describing the house that George Pullman, his wife Hattie, and 10 servants occupied on the avenue that, in 1880, writer and resident Arthur Meeker Jr. called "the sunny street that held the sifted few." Pullman's house, more a statement than a home, has been described as the showiest place on Prairie Avenue. It reflected the lifestyle of a serial entrepreneur. Pullman was the consummate pragmatist, a man whose main mission in life was business success—at any cost. The house he built reflected his multiple business triumphs.

Pullman's house was completed in 1876, having taken almost six years to build. The architect was Henry S. Jaffray, a designer little known in Chicago but with an impressive pedigree, having worked for four years in the late 1850s in the office of New York's most sought-after society architect, Richard Morris Hunt. In 1891 and 1896, at the time the Pullmans' daughters Harriet and Florence each married, Pullman enlarged the house, hiring Solon S. Beman, who had designed Pullman, his factory town south of Chicago. The house grew to contain a 200-seat theater, an organ room decorated in polished white enamel and gold leaf, a dining room with satin brocade walls, an Egyptian room, a billiard room, a palm room, a bowling alley, a conservatory, and multiple parlors.

The prominently sited French Empire-style house was set back from the street and surrounded by lawn. It stood three stories, with the third consisting of a sloping mansard roof topped

CONSERVATORY AND STABLE

by metal cresting. One entered either under an arched porte cochere or a stately raised porch flanked by classical columns. Its glass greenhouse was a large, elegantly designed structure featuring four full-height concave arches. Arthur Miller, Archivist and Librarian for Special Collections at Lake Forest College, has pointed out the importance of gardens and greenhouses to late 19th-century dining and decorating. Joan Morgan and Allison Richardson noted that in cuisine there was a shift from plain cooking to a new French standard focusing on quality ingredients

and beautiful presentation. The ingredients were often grown in family greenhouses. In interior design, the impact of France can be seen in the revival of the lighter palette, gilding and rococo detailing, popular in 18th-century France. This approach was prescribed by A. H. Davenport for the drawing room in Beman's 1891 addition. Exotic plants grown in the conservatory were placed throughout the house.

George Pullman started with little money or, it seemed, opportunity. Born in 1830 in a small town outside Buffalo, New York, he left school at

GREENHOUSE

age 14 to work as a cabinetmaker in his brother's shop. His father, James Lewis Pullman, had invented a machine for transporting buildings on wheels. When he died, George concentrated on the building-moving business to support his mother and several unmarried siblings. In 1857, when business got slow, he visited Chicago in search of more work. His timing was excellent. Pullman arrived just when the marshy city was undertaking a project to raise Chicago's business district by eight feet to accommodate a new sewer system. Pullman secured a contract to raise two

of the city's best-known hotels and achieved a fine reputation raising multistory stone and brick masonry buildings.

Pullman's second success, and the one for which he is universally known, is the development of the Pullman railroad car. Having acquired money from his previous venture, Pullman and his friend New York State Senator Benjamin Field established a luxury-sleeping-car business in 1858. Before Pullman, sleeping coaches were uncomfortable and the food available consisted of stale coffee, bad doughnuts, and hardtack beef.

MAIN STAIRCASE

No trains featured elegant decor or posh restaurants. This all changed in 1864, just as the Civil War was ending. Pullman built a new car, costing $20,000, which he called the *Pioneer*. When President Abraham Lincoln was assassinated in April 1865, it was the *Pioneer* that transported his body back home to Springfield, Illinois. Offering use of the car was but one of several ingenious public relations strategies Pullman used to build his company.

After the Pullman Company was incorporated in 1867, its savvy owner introduced numerous services never seen before. Pullman began by calling his business Pullman's Palace Car Company, using the term *palace cars* to describe those for sleeping and dining. He developed and marketed the first hotel on wheels, consisting of a sleeper with an attached kitchen and dining car. And the food on palace cars was superb. In 1868, he built a train he called the *Delmonico*, featuring elegant cuisine and cleverly named for the famous New York restaurant. In addition, Pullman's train cars had accordion connectors between cars, to keep down noise and wind, and

ENTRY HALL LOOKING INTO PARLOR

STUDY

DINING ROOM

DRAWING ROOM

sleeping compartments fitted with fine linens. These were the most elaborate train cars anyone had ever seen. To provide first-class treatment, Pullman hired recently freed house slaves to serve as porters. Although he provided many employment opportunities for blacks, he paid them smaller salaries than white men would have commanded and he was criticized in the press for demoralizing his employees.

In 1880, after years of enjoying great economic success, Pullman purchased 3,500 acres and established the town of Pullman, 14 miles south of the city (today within Chicago's corporate limits). His company town had everything but saloons (as Pullman didn't want his employees getting drunk and disorderly)—its own shopping center, bank, theater, church, schools, parks, and library, as well as the Florence Hotel and housing for more than 10,000 people. But residents were totally beholden to Pullman, required to rent their houses with no option to purchase them. The church remained empty because no one could afford the rent Pullman demanded. He provided water and gas, but his employees had to pay a ten

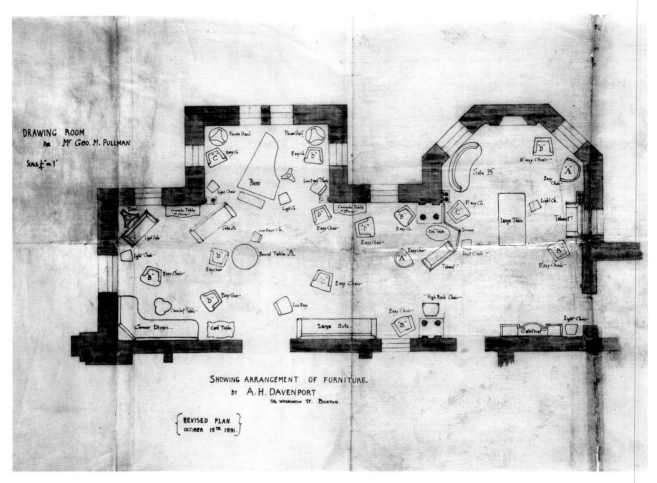

FURNITURE PLAN OF DRAWING ROOM

percent premium. There was no local governing body to allow the opportunity to express grievances. Unions were kept out and strikes were not tolerated. Pullman retained control over all aspects of the residents' lives.

Pullman's company enjoyed great success, both in the United States and abroad. It produced more than 2,000 palace cars that could accommodate 100,000 nightly. Pullman had no trouble attracting investors, including Andrew Carnegie. All went relatively well until the depression of 1893, which lasted four years and caused a significant decline in the company's business. To lower costs, Pullman cut his employees' wages by 30 percent, yet he refused

to reduce their rents. And he allowed no option for negotiation, as paying off his investors took precedence over paying his workers. Employees were predictably furious and called in the American Railway Union, led by Eugene Debs: on May 11, 1894, they went on strike. Violence broke out, Pullman called in federal troops, and, when shooting ensued, more than 30 people were killed. The Pullman Strike remains infamous in American labor history.

In 1897, Pullman died of a massive coronary. Fearful that his angry employees would desecrate his body, Pullman specified how he wanted to be buried. His casket was placed in a space that was 13 feet long, 9 feet wide, and 8 feet deep, filled

CONSERVATORY

with concrete and covered by railroad ties. Pullman's tomb, designed by his company architect Solon S. Beman, is marked by a single tall Corinthian column. He was buried at night in Graceland Cemetery. The American satirist Ambrose Bierce said, "It is clear the family in their bereavement was making sure the sonofabitch wasn't going to get up and come back." In 1921, following the death of Hattie, Pullman's wife, the palace he called home was demolished.

EDWARD UIHLEIN HOUSE

2041 WEST PIERCE AVENUE

FROMMANN & JEBSEN, 1877

VIEW FROM PIERCE AVENUE

CONSERVATORY

THE STORY of Edward Uihlein reflects the pioneer spirit that characterized many 19th-century men who went to Chicago to seek their fortunes. Like other Chicagoans, he left Europe, established a successful business, started a family, and built a large, interesting house that expressed his success and personal taste. In this case, it also expressed his fascination with horticulture.

Edward G. Uihlein was born in 1845 in Wertheim-am-Main, Germany, where his parents operated a small inn that served the Main River trade. They had hoped their son would become a Roman Catholic priest but respected his desire to enter business and found him a job in his mother's nearby hometown, Miltenberg, as an apprentice in a general store. When an opportunity arose for him to join his two elder brothers in the United States, they got him released from his apprenticeship and encouraged him to leave.

At age 19, Edward arrived in the United States via New York City. He stopped in Milwaukee to visit his uncle, named Krug, who had a modest

FRONT PORCH DETAIL

brewery there. He then left for St. Louis and went to work for a business that supplied oil and wagon parts. Three years later, in 1867, seeing opportunities for his firm, he moved to Chicago to open a branch operation. By then, his uncle had died and his aunt, who inherited the business, had married the company bookkeeper, Joseph Schlitz, who changed the brewery's name to Schlitz. When Chicago's great fire of 1871 had destroyed almost all of the city's brewing capacity and the company had more orders than it could handle, Schlitz approached Uihlein to work for him. Uihlein opened a Chicago office of Schlitz Brewing and, in time, was responsible for all the Schlitz beer that left Milwaukee. Schlitz beer was heavily promoted

at the World's Columbian Exposition of 1893, with the slogan "The beer that made Milwaukee famous." The terra-cotta globe trademark can still be found on several buildings in Chicago that once were Schlitz taverns.

In 1875, Edward Uihlein married Augusta Manns of the Wheaton area. Two years later, he purchased several lots north and west of the neighborhoods where most of Chicago's wealthy families had settled, in an area that soon became known as Wicker Park. Land was available, labor was plentiful, and building materials were cheap. The house's total construction cost in 1877 was $10,000 (almost $200,000 in 2006 dollars). Wicker Park became a neighborhood of families from all

PARLOR

walks of life. It developed as a community of modest houses for blue-collar workers and mansions built by several of Chicago's wealthy Swedish and German Americans. The Uihleins had five children; two of their daughters married into the Conrad Seipp family, who were also in the brewing industry.

The Uihlein House was comfortable—not pretentious like the houses built during the 1870s for George Pullman, Cyrus McCormick, and Marshall Field. Those residences displayed a grandeur of scale and lavishness of detail not present here. Although the Uihlein house was tall and stately with a mansard roof, typical of many houses built during the Victorian period, it was graced by porches and balconies. Inside, the decorative details included fretwork in the doorways separating rooms, statues on pedestals, and knick-knacks, but the wall and ceiling surfaces were not all covered with paneling or applied ornament. The furnishings were not resplendent, not chosen to impress. The house looked lived-in.

For their architect, the Uihleins selected Emil Frommann of Frommann & Jebsen. In 1895, perhaps because of Uihlein's influence, the firm designed the old Stable and Refectory in Chicago's Humboldt Park. In 1905, Frommann's firm built Schlitz Row, a series of flats and taverns bearing the terra-cotta globe Schlitz trademark, near the then suburb of Pullman. In an

PARLOR DETAIL

attempt to keep his company town dry, George Pullman controlled the surrounding land. After a court order required him to sell off some of his local real-estate holdings, Uihlein purchased 10 acres and filled them with housing, taverns, beer gardens, and stables that were not controlled by the Pullman Company. The brick buildings Frommann & Jebsen designed were reminiscent of 19th-century German industrial towns.

The glory of the Uihlein house lay in its voluptuous garden and its exotic conservatory, built in 1888. Uihlein's passion was horticulture. The Victorians were notorious for collecting and Uihlein acquired plants. He amassed a notable array of tropical palms and orchids from all over the world and built his large domed conservatory to house as many rare plants and palms as it could accommodate. His collection included 5,000 of the world's rarest orchids. The structure was far more than a greenhouse; it was known as the largest private conservatory in Chicago. The 1911 issue of *Who's Who in Chicago* states that his collections were considered among the best in the United States. Typically, his successful contemporaries listed their hobbies as golf or riding; Uihlein's were listed as gardening and horticulture.

Uihlein was active in the World's Columbian Exposition, furnishing many of the flowers and shrubs displayed in Horticulture Hall. In 1894, Governor John Peter Altgeld appointed Uihlein as a commissioner of Chicago's West Park System, and he served until a Republican succeeded Altgeld in 1896. While a West Park commissioner, Uihlein made several trips to Jamaica and the West Indies, at his own expense, to purchase hundreds of speci-mens of rare plants. In 1904, Uihlein became president of the Chicago Horticultural Society.

Because the enactment of Prohibition in 1919 adversely affected many members of the Uihlein family, Uihlein's surviving children elected to demolish the house and its conservatory shortly after Edward Uihlein's death in 1921.

CYRUS McCORMICK JR. HOUSE

50 EAST HURON STREET

ARCHITECT UNKNOWN, EARLY 1880s

ADDITION BY SHEPLEY, RUTAN & COOLIDGE, 1910

VIEW FROM HURON STREET

ENTRY AND STAIR HALL

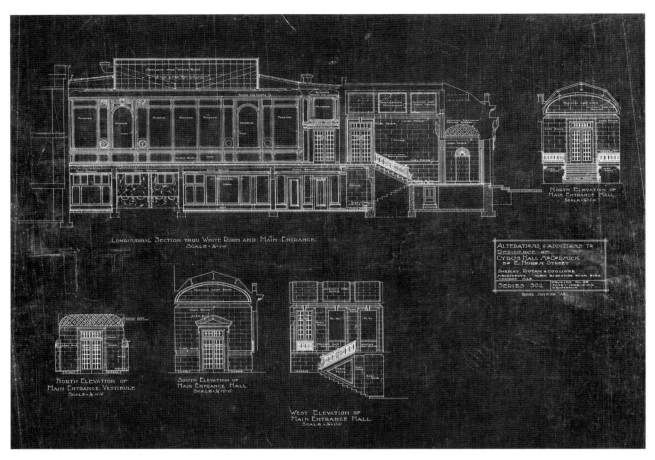

CROSS-SECTION DRAWINGS OF ADDITION BY SHEPLEY, RUTAN, & COOLIDGE, 1910

CYRUS MCCORMICK JR. was the son of Cyrus Hall McCormick, whose invention of the reaper revolutionized farming. Cyrus Jr. guided the company that his father founded through the harvester wars, fierce competition between a number of small companies that eventually merged to become International Harvester, with himself. as the president.

In 1884, when his father died, Cyrus Hall McCormick took over the leadership of the McCormick Harvesting Machine Company. He was only 25 years old. Although he had graduated first in his high school class, attended Princeton, and been well trained in the farm-implement-manufacturing business by his father, Cyrus could not have anticipated the immense labor issues he would have to resolve. His company employees, like steel and textile workers, labored long hours. McCormick's 1,300 men worked 10-hour shifts, six days a week, and their efforts to restore cut wages turned to violence in 1883. The May 4, 1886 *New York Times* reported, "There was a collision at McCormick's Reaper Works, between a mob of 7,000 or 8,000 Anarchist workmen and tramps, maddened with free beer and free speech, and a squad of policemen." In actuality, the situation was far more complex. McCormick's workers had, in 1885, endured considerable repression, and attempts by his unionized workers to negotiate were met with refusals. A strike resulted and McCormick used Pinkerton detectives and strikebreakers to

STAIR LANDING AND DOOR TO TAPESTRY ROOM IN ADDITION

try to overcome the union. Nettie McCormick, Cyrus Jr.'s mother, chastised her son for his handling of the 1885 strike and recalled to him the old days, when workers and management enjoyed pleasant relations. The strike of 1886 resulted in more than 500 shots fired and hundreds of broken factory windows. Despite attempts by Cyrus Jr. to ameliorate the situation with concessions, the friction escalated into violence and death. The next day a rally culminated in Chicago's Haymarket Riot—the 19th century's most infamous labor confrontation.

Until 1902, Cyrus McCormick Jr. served as president of the McCormick Harvesting Machine Company. He then presided over the successful consolidation of his company with four others, including the Deering Harvester Company and Warder, Bushnell & Glessner, into International Harvester. Under his leadership as president, then chairman (until 1935), International Harvester became the world's largest manufacturer of farm machinery, with assets of $400 million, 50,000-plus employees, and plants all over the world. It became the company that perfected the reaper Cyrus' father invented and expanded it to provide other products and services. The firm initiated scientific training for farmers, engaged in research on crops and soil, produced tractors and

TAPESTRY ROOM

trucks, and diversified into items not associated with farming.

Cyrus McCormick Jr. built his house in the 1880s on Chicago's near north side in "McCormickville," the area centered on Huron and Rush streets, where many other members of the McCormick family lived. Two generations of McCormicks had built houses in the neighborhood. The grandest, constructed in 1875–79, belonged to Cyrus Sr.

The house Cyrus Jr. shared with his wife Harriet, until her death in 1921, and with their children was typical of the period. Faced in stone, it stood three stories and was capped by a

mansard roof. The eclecticism of the period prevailed on the interior, with gothic strapwork forming the ceiling of the grand wood-paneled stair hall and classical treatments in the Empire room. A list of furnishings purchased from an antiquities dealer in Florence, Italy, notes several cabinets, chairs, torchères, andirons, and candleholders dating from the 15th to 17th centuries. The McCormicks' art collection included paintings in the library and dining room by George Inness and John Constable. The house's most elegant space, however, was an addition designed by the Boston architectural firm of Shepley, Rutan & Coolidge in 1910. Reached by a grand marble

LADIES' DRESSING ROOM BY DAVID ADLER, 1928

staircase, it was referred to as the Tapestry Room and featured a musicians' balcony. In 1928, society architect David Adler remodeled the men's and women's dressing rooms.

Cyrus McCormick Jr. moved from his house in McCormickville after his second marriage to Alice Holt, who had been his private secretary. They retained a townhouse at Astor Street and Burton Place on the Gold Coast and a country place, named Walden, in Lake Forest. He died of a heart attack in 1936, leaving an estate of $18

million to his wife and children, as well as to Presbyterian charities and Princeton University.

Of the many McCormick family residences, today only a double house built in 1875 by Leander McCormick (the brother of Cyrus Sr.) and his son Robert Hall McCormick remains. A fragment of the residence of L. Hamilton McCormick, a cousin of Cyrus Jr., can be seen behind a remodeled restaurant facade. Cyrus Jr.'s house, like his father's, has been demolished.

JOSEPH SEARS HOUSE

1815 PRAIRIE AVENUE

DANIEL H. BURNHAM, 1881–82

ARTHUR HEUN (REMODELING), IN 1902, FOR ARTHUR MEEKER SR.

VIEW FROM PRAIRIE AVENUE

HOUSE AS REMODELED FOR ARTHUR MEEKER SR.

THE HOUSE at 1815 Prairie Avenue was built in 1881 for Joseph Sears, who became important in the history of Chicago as the developer of the suburb of Kenilworth. For his Prairie Avenue architect, Sears chose the young and not yet famous Daniel Hudson Burnham. The three-story house was faced with yellow Lemont limestone and had a slate mansard roof. On the north, a driveway led to stables behind the house. To the south, Sears had a log cabin built as a playhouse for his children.

Sears and his father, John, founded the Chicago branch of the Swedenborgian Church, the Church of the New Jerusalem. The Chicago members formed a closely knit social group, and it was through the church that Sears and Burnham became friends.

Joseph Sears was born in Lockport, Illinois, in 1843. His family was said to have descended from the Pilgrims who landed on Plymouth Rock. In 1848 his parents moved to Chicago and Joseph's father entered the wholesale drug business. His father's company, Ball & Sears, expanded into manufacturing oil, lard, and candles and was bought by Fairbank, Peck & Company, who made soap from lard supplied by the city's meatpacking industry.

Joseph Sears attended the Dearborn School, the first permanent public school built in Chicago, and later Bell's Commercial College. At 21, he entered the army and he served during the Civil War. Afterwards, Sears married Helen Stedman Berry of Chicago and went to work for N. K. Fairbank & Company, renamed after it was purchased by the American Cotton Oil Company. Under Joseph Sears, N. K. Fairbank & Company developed Cottolene, a cottonseed-oil substitute for cooking lard. It was a great success. The company

ENTRY HALL

was known for its household products: Gold Dust Twins Washing Powder and the famous Santa Claus soaps and Fairy soaps, which were packaged with promotional picture trading cards popular with children. N. K. Fairbank & Company grew to 1,000 employees, with branches in St. Louis and Omaha. Their products were exported to England, Europe, and Central and South America.

The Sears family lived at five different addresses on Prairie Avenue, moving successively north until 1879, when they purchased the land for their house at 1815 Prairie. They lived for a short while at 1919 Prairie in Marshall Field Jr.'s house. This was directly next to the Marshall Field

residence. The house had been built by William Murray and bought by Marshall Field for his son. Murray was the father-in-law of Arthur Meeker Sr., who bought the Sears house after Sears moved to Kenilworth, the suburb he founded and developed. Sears moved to the North Shore in 1893, and his house was rented for a year to Clayton J. Beechman, who was in the lumber business. From 1895 to 1901, Levy Mayer, a Yale-educated corporate lawyer, occupied the house, which was sold to Arthur Meeker Sr. in 1902.

Arthur Meeker and his wife, who purchased the Sears house, had been living in London, where he managed overseas meat distribution for

DINING ROOM

Armour & Company. He was called back to Chicago to take over as second-in-command of Armour's meatpacking operations. When he bought the Sears house, Meeker hired Arthur Heun, an up-and-coming young residential architect, to remodel the structure. In 1893, Heun had taken over Francis Whitehouse's practice after working on houses for Whitehouse's prominent clients. The January 1906 *Architectural Record* described Heun as a "younger architect whose work is worth attention both for the good taste and skill which it embodies and its relation to the most significant tendencies in current Western domestic architecture." Heun removed the exterior stone stairway at the north side of the house and replaced it with a ground-level entry vestibule. He also removed Burnham's square corner bay and replaced it with a new projecting two-story rectangular bay at the front of the house.

The novelist Arthur Meeker Jr. was born at 1815 Prairie the year the Meekers moved in. Vivid descriptions of growing up on Prairie Avenue and of Chicago society are contained in his novel *Prairie Avenue* and in his memoir, *Chicago with Love.* Meeker also recalled architect Arthur Heun, whom the children disliked. He had "a round bullet head, a high squalling voice, and a propensity to pat and poke," although he did give

LIVING ROOM

the Meeker children exquisitely wrapped Christmas gifts. In the absence of interior photos of Heun's remodeling, we have Arthur Meeker Jr.'s descriptions:

> The stairs that had been banished from the facade now led upward inside the front hall to a second hall, upon which three rooms (the library, dining room and drawing room) gave (opened) . . . Halfway up the stairs to the first bedroom floor there was a small side gallery that commanded the drawing room . . . . It was here that the children were allowed to sit looking down at the guests during the Meekers' frequent parties.

A stairway led from his sister's bedroom to a playroom with a rooftop sandbox that overlooked, through a window, the house's squash court. The Meekers' remodeling, which had been one of Heun's first projects, led to commissions for the family's summer house in Lake Forest and the huge Italian-style villa Heun designed in 1908 for J. Ogden Armour in Lake Forest.

The Meekers lived on Prairie Avenue for 11 years before abandoning the south side as many wealthy Chicagoans were doing. In 1913, Meeker and J. Ogden Armour, whose city house was on South Michigan Avenue, bought the entire frontage on Lake Shore Drive between Barry and Wellington streets, 350 feet facing the lake. The Meekers commissioned New York architect

CARRIAGE OUTING: MRS. ARTHUR CATON (SECOND MRS. MARSHALL FIELD, FAR LEFT), FRANKLIN MacVEAGH, MRS. ARTHUR MEEKER, AND ARTHUR MEEKER SR. (ON FAR RIGHT)

Charles Platt to design a townhouse for them. Their move this far north was thought unfashionable at the time, and Chicagoans began referring to the area as Meekerville.

As an indication of how dramatically Prairie Avenue was changing, by the time the Meekers left this onetime bastion of Chicago society, it was being converted to commercial and industrial use. In 1914, the Meekers sold the house on 1815 Prairie Avenue to the D. C. Heath Publishing Company, which used it as its Chicago office. In 1966, the Heath company sold the house to printers R. R. Donnelley & Sons. It was demolished the following year.

JOHN WESLEY DOANE HOUSE

1827 Prairie Avenue

Theodore V. Wadskier, 1882

PRAIRIE AVENUE ELEVATION

VIEW FROM PRAIRIE AVENUE

JOHN WESLEY DOANE'S house was often referred to as "Chicago's First Palace," a response to author Everett Chamberlin (*Chicago and Its Suburbs*, 1874), who wrote that there were no palaces in the "secluded and sedate precincts of Prairie Avenue." The house's opulence was nationally recognized. Photographs of its interiors were among those of only three Chicago residences featured in *Artistic Houses* (1883), a three-volume set

of books by G. W. Sheldon, better known as the author of the influential publication *Artistic Country Seats* (1886), a selection of America's great country houses.

Doane's house was remarkable not only for its splendor but for its use of the most modern technologies. Completed in 1882, the house was the first in Chicago to be illuminated by electricity. Doane was a founder of the Western Edison Light

STAIR HALL

Company (later Commonwealth Edison) and had a high-speed Armington & Sims engine and a belted Edison shunt-wound generator installed in the basement of his coach house, with underground pipes connecting to the main house. The generator could power 558 Edison light bulbs.

Doane celebrated the house's completion and his silver wedding anniversary with a party for 400 people held on November 10, 1882. The *Chicago Tribune* described the party as a "brilliant social event . . . Mr. Doane has recently completed what is probably the finest house West of New York, and it was fit that he should inaugurate it by a celebration of his silver wedding anniversary . . .

the interior of the house is as exquisitely rich as taste and art can make it, and last night it presented a scene of grandeur and beauty rarely witnessed . . . Mr. Doane has illuminated his house with 250 of the Edison electric incandescent lights, and they made the house brilliant in the extreme." The description continued, "From the curb to the door of the vestibule there was spread an awning lighted up with electric lamps . . . The elaborate mantel of the parlor was hidden by banks of exquisite flowers while from out of the brass hearths in all the rooms and halls shone forth electric lights, so arranged as to imitate a glowing fire." The guest list included Chicago's most prominent families.

PARLOR AND STAIR HALL

Shortly after Doane's party, his Prairie Avenue neighbors Marshall Field, Edison Keith, Joseph Sears, and Thomas Dent (the attorney for the Chicago Board of Trade) all had their houses wired for electricity, supplied by Doane's generator.

The Doanes, like many of their Prairie Avenue neighbors, often entertained on a grand scale. One story has it that, after two hundred people attended a concert by Ignacy Paderewski held at the house, the musician joined Doane and his friends and played cards until morning, then lost the fee he had been paid for his concert.

John Wesley Doane was born in 1833 in Thompson, Connecticut. At the age of 22 he went west to Chicago, arriving in 1855. He rented a grocery store which, in a span of 15 years, became the city's largest, with sales of $3 million. Doane's store, however, was completely wiped out by the great Chicago fire of 1871. A year later he had started a new business as a direct importer of tea and coffee, completely bypassing East Coast markets and making a second fortune. He was also involved in a number of other successful commercial and banking ventures. In addition to forming the Western Edison Light Company along with Thomas Edison and 10 other Chicagoans, Doane served as president of the Merchants' Loan and Trust Company and as a

HALL DETAIL

director of the Pullman Palace Car Company. He was a founder and president of the prestigious Commercial Club of Chicago and a trustee of St. Luke's Free Hospital. Instrumental in securing the rights to hold the 1893 World's Fair in Chicago, Doane was one of three Chicagoans who together offered the U.S. Senate a $5 million guaranty that Chicago could raise the funds to put on the exposition.

Doane's architect was Theodore Vigo Wadskier, who was born in the Danish West Indies and educated in Copenhagen. He worked in New York and Philadelphia before going to Chicago in 1857. A designer of schools and churches, he also built houses for wealthy Chicago patrons and was known for the personal attention he gave to clients' needs. The house he designed for John and Julia Moulton Doane and their two daughters was French châteauesque in style with a mansard roof and corner tower. The interiors of the ground-floor rooms were paneled in fine woods: oak, Santo Domingo mahogany, and bird's-eye maple. The

entry vestibule had stained-glass windows made by John La Farge. The grand entry hall and stairway were Eastlake in style and recall Richard Morris Hunt's 1872 remodeling of Chateau-sur-Mer in Newport. Doane's house, in addition to being the first Chicago residence with electric lights, had its own laundry facilities, which were described in a *Chicago Tribune* article as the "most complete in a private dwelling, with steam boilers and steam drying racks in the basement; the steam [was] furnished from an engine and boilers in the barn behind the house."

Besides his Prairie Avenue house, Doane had an apartment in New York and a summer house in his birthplace of Thompson, Connecticut. In 1898, after the Western Edison Company was dissolved to form the Chicago Edison Company, Doane moved his family to New York, where he could pursue other financial interests. Doane died in 1901 and the Prairie Avenue house was sold. It was ravaged by fire on January 15, 1927, and then razed.

SAMUEL M. NICKERSON HOUSE
40 East Erie Street
Burling & Whitehouse, 1883

VIEW FROM ERIE STREET

EAST FACADE

SAMUEL M. NICKERSON, who epito-
mized the entrepreneurial spirit of the
transplanted Yankee, built one of Chicago's most
beautiful houses. Born in 1830 in Chatham,
Massachusetts, Nickerson went west penniless but
eager to find his fortune in the burgeoning
metropolis. He arrived in 1858 and, when he had
the funds, purchased a distillery at a time when
Chicago's consumption of alcohol was legendary.
Sales soared, especially during the Civil War when
alcohol was used to manufacture explosives.
Nickerson's success allowed him to retire from the
liquor business and shift his interests to banking.
He served several terms as president of Chicago's
First National Bank and helped organize the
Union Stock-Yards National Bank. He also served

seven years as president of the Chicago City
Horse Railroad Company.

Like many of Chicago's successful young businessmen—including steel magnate Joseph
Ryerson and dry-goods entrepreneur Levi Leiter,
Marshall Field's partner—Nickerson purchased
land in what later came to be called
McCormickville, where many members of the
prestigious McCormick family lived. After the
1871 fire, this then-quiet residential neighborhood
just north of the Chicago River was, along with
Prairie Avenue, considered very fashionable.

Nickerson hired Edward Burling of the firm of
Burling & Whitehouse to design one of the city's
most elegant houses remaining from this period.
Completed in 1883, Nickerson's masonry

STAIR HALL

mansion, sheathed in gray limestone and sandstone, took three years to build. Its blocklike simplicity, classical portico, and bracketed cornice suggest an Italian palazzo. It is said to have cost $450,000, not including furnishings.

The house's exterior is restrained, but that appearance belies a lavish interior. Its solid construction was necessary to support the weight of marble, for the house is a confection of multicolored onyx, alabaster, and, in the stair hall alone, more than 20 varieties of Italian, Belgian, and American marble. Colors range from pale red Verona to dark green with white veining. Exotic

woods, including primavera and ebony as well as mahogany, oak, pine, and maple, were used for paneling and patterned floors to create a different look in each of the house's 28 rooms. The February 1883 issue of *Inland Architect* declared that the interior decoration, executed by Burling in collaboration with A. Fiedler of New York, "reached a standard of elegance never before attained in Chicago."

Classical order and detailing modulates the richness of the interior of the Nickerson house, yet its glamour and opulence were equaled by only a handful of contemporary Chicago mansions, including the Potter Palmer and George Pullman houses.

LIBRARY AND ART GALLERY

Like other wealthy Chicagoans, Nickerson was a patron of the arts and a serious art collector—some have called him a latter-day Medici. Although paintings and sculptures were located throughout the house, most of his collection, including works by George Inness, Thomas Cole, and Albert Bierstadt, as well as prints, drawings, and Chinese and Japanese porcelains in glass cases, was housed in a large gallery in the house's north-west corner.

Nickerson, his wife, and their only son, Roland, lived in the house with a staff of 11. In 1900, the Nickersons moved to New York. Samuel

Nickerson then donated his art collection, along with a $50,000 endowment, to the Art Institute of Chicago, where he had served as a trustee since the museum's incorporation in 1879.

The second owner of this house, Lucius G. Fisher, was president of Union Bag and Paper Company. He is best known for having built the famous Chicago School skyscraper bearing his name. An avid hunter, Fisher transformed the art gallery into a game room for his hunting trophies and his rare-book collection. The remodeling, designed by noted Prairie School architect George Maher, included a prominent fireplace incorporating

FIRST FLOOR RECEPTION ROOM

GAME ROOM, 1901

SECOND FLOOR HALL

large lion heads, iridescent glazed tiles, and a Tiffany lamp with hunting motifs hanging from the glass-domed ceiling. In 1953, the Fisher collection of animal heads was donated to the Chicago Board of Education.

After Fisher died in 1919, several of Chicago's most influential citizens purchased the Nickerson house and donated it to the American College of Surgeons to be used as their headquarters. In 1922–26, the porte cochere and first-floor conservatory were removed and replaced with the John B. Murphy Memorial Auditorium, constructed for the College of Surgeons and designed by the dis-

tinguished Chicago architectural firm of Marshall & Fox. During the 1990s, the mansion served as home to the Richard Love Galleries.

After an extensive and careful restoration done between 2003 and 2007, the Nickerson house has opened its doors as the Richard H. Driehaus Museum. A highly respected Chicagoan, Mr. Driehaus has received international recognition for his contributions to historic preservation. Original Nickerson and Fisher furnishings, as well as objects selected from the Driehaus collection, are displayed to portray the house as it looked between 1883 and 1919.

ERIE STREET ELEVATION AND PLAN

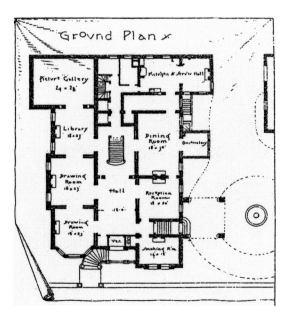

GROUND FLOOR PLAN

EDITH ROCKEFELLER McCORMICK HOUSE

1000 LAKE SHORE DRIVE

SOLON S. BEMAN, 1883

BELLEVUE PLACE FACADE

VIEW FROM LAKE SHORE DRIVE

E DITH ROCKEFELLER MCCORMICK, an intelligent, complex, enigmatic, and thoroughly fascinating woman, was the daughter of oil tycoon John D. Rockefeller. She married Harold F. McCormick, son of Cyrus McCormick, the prosperous head of the McCormick Harvesting Machine Company. Her extravagance knew no bounds and her dinners were legendary. She was a patron of the opera and of literature, donating more than $5 million dollars to the Chicago Civic Opera and providing funds for James Joyce to publish *A Portrait of the Artist as a Young Man*. And she was a woman of high intellect, who studied with Dr. Carl Jung and became a lay analyst.

She was born Edith Rockefeller in 1872 in Cleveland, Ohio, and moved to New York as a teenager. Intellectual pursuits fascinated her, and she played the cello, became fluent in several languages, and read voraciously. Although her father was one of the richest men in America, frugality was forced on her. She was also protected from exposure to the public, educated by tutors at home until she was sent to boarding school.

Edith Rockefeller's life changed dramatically when she met Harold McCormick, a handsome college friend of her brother. On November 26, 1896, she and McCormick married at the Fifth Avenue Baptist Church in New York City. Shortly

BELLEVUE PLACE GATE

afterward, the McCormicks moved to Council Bluffs, Iowa, where Harold was sent to manage the western branch of his family company. After two years, they moved to Chicago and settled into a 41-room mansion at the corner of Bellevue and Lake Shore Drive, where they lived with 17 servants.

The McCormicks' newly acquired house, designed by architect Solon S. Beman, was reputed to have been a gift from Edith's millionaire father, a story she denied. The house was built in the 1880s by Nathaniel S. Jones, a successful grain merchant, and then owned by another early wealthy Chicagoan, Joseph T. Torrence, who had started a system of belt-line railroads to handle freight.

In 1898, the McCormicks moved into their house on Lake Shore Drive, and Mrs. McCormick set about furnishing the house with great pieces such as a Louis XV dressing table and chairs, a gilt dinner service presented by Napoléon to his sister Pauline Borghese, and a Persian rug said to have been owned by Peter the Great. The well-known Chicago interior decorator Cornelia Conger commented that the house "reeked formality" and that her client never really had a flair for putting pieces together. The fine things were used for state occasions, as when Mrs. McCormick hosted the Princess of Sweden or the Queen of Romania.

ENTRY HALL

EMPIRE ROOM

NAPOLEON ROOM

At her funeral, Mrs. McCormick's staff remembered her as a perfect mistress, easy to work for and uncomplaining. She led her life with formality and routine verging on ritual. Her footman said she never spoke to the staff; all directions were given through Baxter, the head butler. Four men were required to serve even the simplest luncheon for two. Her pre-opera dinners were said to have been timed by a jeweled clock to last 35 minutes, and guests were rushed out to ensure Edith would be in her box before the opening curtain. She reigned over her parties as royalty, often donning either a diamond choker and matching tiara or Catherine the Great of Russia's jewels, said to have

been worth $2 million. Respecting the wishes of her father, she never served alcohol. Beginning in the early 1900s, when Bertha Palmer was spending more and more time away from Chicago, in Newport and Sarasota, Edith Rockefeller McCormick became the unchallenged queen of Chicago society.

The McCormicks had five children, but only three survived beyond early childhood. As a memorial to their first son, John D. Rockefeller McCormick, who died from scarlet fever at age four, Edith established the John McCormick Institute for Infectious Diseases, where a cure for the illness was discovered.

DINING ROOM

Following the deaths of her children, Mrs. McCormick fell into a severe depression, and in 1913 she left with her husband for Switzerland to seek treatment from famed psychoanalyst Carl Jung. The trip had been scheduled for two months but lasted eight years. During that time, while his wife was establishing an analytical practice, studying comparative religions and philosophy, and adding Sanskrit to her linguistic repertoire, Harold McCormick went back to work at International Harvester in Chicago. He eventually began an affair with opera singer Ganna Walska, whom she subsequently married. Despite their divorce, Edith and Harold McCormick remained warm friends.

Edith McCormick returned to Chicago in 1921. During the 1920s, she developed a thriving psychoanalytic practice that attracted her socialite friends. She also continued her philanthropy, donating acreage in Riverside, Illinois, to establish the Chicago Zoological Gardens. She had returned to the city with Edwin H. Krenn, an architect she met while studying with Jung. They became great companions, taking meals and attending opera and the cinema together, and later were partners in a real estate business with a Swiss friend of Krenn's, Ernest A. Dato. Their business focused on creating affordable-housing subdivisions and modestly priced apartment buildings. However, the firm

BUTLER'S PANTRY

began losing money, and when McCormick understood her tenants' predicament she let collection of rent and mortgage payments slip by.

In 1928, New York society architect Charles Platt, who had designed a country house in Lake Forest for the McCormicks, designed an enormous palazzo-style city house for Edith. Although construction drawings were completed, the house was never built. It was Edith's intention for it to be donated after her death to the City of Chicago and subdivided for use as a mayor's residence and a municipal art museum.

Even as her wealth diminished, Edith Rockefeller McCormick led the life of the grande dame, providing glittering stories for the society columns. By 1932, however, she had lost so much money that her father and her brother John D. Rockefeller Jr. insisted that she move from her Lake Shore Drive mansion into a suite at the Drake Hotel, where she eventually died. Her lavish mansion on Chicago's Gold Coast was opened one last time for her funeral service held in the house's Empire Room. After her death, the house served as a school and in 1953 was demolished to be replaced by a high-rise apartment building. Mrs. McCormick's friend Arthur Meeker Jr. commented in a 1965 newspaper article, "Mrs. McCormick's death marked the end of an era. No one again could afford to live as she lived—nor perhaps, even if they could, would they have wanted to."

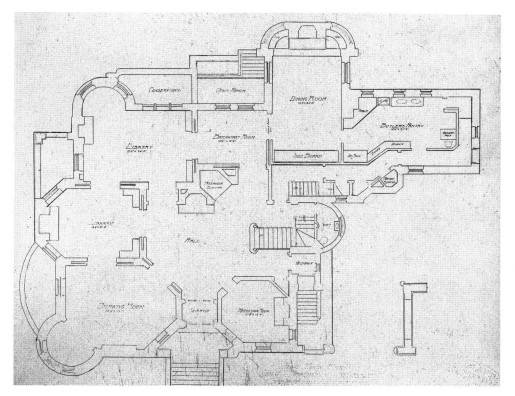

FIRST FLOOR PLAN

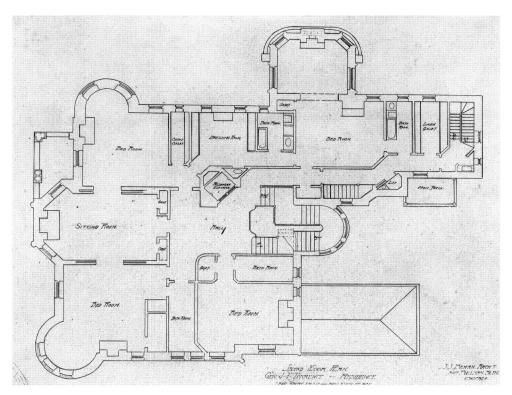

SECOND FLOOR PLAN

SAMUEL EBERLY GROSS HOUSE

(FORMERLY JAMES CHARNLEY)

1204 LAKE SHORE DRIVE

BURNHAM & ROOT, 1883–87

DIVISION STREET FACADE

CORNER OF DIVISION STREET AND LAKE SHORE DRIVE

I N 1887, Samuel E. Gross, one of Chicago's most successful developers of residential subdivisions, purchased a house on Chicago's Lake Shore Drive. He bought the house from its original owners, James and Helen Charnley, who lived there for only four years before deciding to build a new house on Asto Street. Perhaps the Charnleys wished to leave the house because of the deaths of their two daughters, ages four and six, during the family's first year there.

The house, designed by architect John W. Root of Burnham & Root, was one of the first to be built on Lake Shore Drive. Begun at the same time as Potter Palmer's "castle," it was complete well before the Palmers moved in, making the Charnleys the area's first residents. At the time, Lake Shore Drive was open land, and Burnham and Root designed a freestanding house more picturesquely suburban in nature than their later city houses, many of which were party-wall structures.

The house had a stone foundation with a brick exterior to comply with the city's postfire requirements forbidding wood construction. Decorative slate tiles in a diagonal pattern sheathed the second floor, and the ground floor was wrapped by an elaborate one-story wooden porch in the Queen Anne style with a chinoiserie railing and slender sets of paired columns. The porch provided views and caught the cool lake breezes in Chicago's hot, humid summers. Above, a second-floor sleeping porch faced east to the lake.

The new owners, the Grosses, lavishly redecorated the house and set about establishing a place for themselves in Chicago society. The remodeling must have been done quickly, because a short time after they bought the house, the *Chicago Tribune* society column for December 3, 1887, announced that Mrs. Samuel Eberly Gross would receive guests there on Tuesday, December 21, from 4:00 until 7:00 p.m. and thereafter on Mondays. The

{ 111 }

EGYPTIAN ROOM

dining room, as well as Samuel's den and library, was furnished in Victorian style, with the wall of the den covered in brown leather with gold stenciling. The music room and Mrs. Gross's bedroom were completely redone in the Louis XVI style, including furniture and decorative millwork. Tiffany-glass windows ornamented the music room, with a composition depicting music installed over their upright piano. The Grosses' Egyptian room featured tones of green, red, and yellow, and had cartouches of the pharaohs displayed in a frieze just below the ceiling. Egyptian-style wood screens covered the windows; a lotus motif decorated the ceiling, and a light fixture featuring four opalescent globes hanging from metal serpents and sacred ibises lit the room.

In *History of Chicago*, edited by Joseph Kirkland and John Moses (1895), the authors suggest that the name of Samuel Eberly Gross had become a household word, "indissolubly associated in the mind of the public with many great enterprises, which have not only added to the city's

LIBRARY

greatness, but have also placed comfortable homes within reach of the industrial classes."

Samuel Gross was born in 1843 in Dauphin, Pennsylvania; he was the great-grandson of a Revolutionary-War captain. In 1846, he moved with his family to Illinois. He served in the army during the Civil War, then settled in Chicago, where he studied at the Union College of Law. After graduating, he bought several lots, constructed houses, and began his career in real-estate development. Energetic and flamboyant, Gross referred to himself

as "the world's greatest real estate promoter." He sold lots on Chicago's west side that could be purchased, on time, for $100. To get prospective buyers to his developments, he often arranged free transportation. In 1890, Gross was selling as many as 500 lots a week and reportedly 3,000 people a day visiting his properties by train. By 1894, according to a biographer, he had sold 40,000 lots, built 8,000 houses, and become a multimillionaire. Today, Gross is best remembered as the developer of Alta Vista Terrace, a one-block-long street of picturesque,

DINING ROOM

MUSIC ROOM

highly prized two-story row houses. These have been restored by their owners and the street has been designated a Chicago landmark.

Gross was an amateur playwright and believed his play *The Merchant Prince of Cornville* to have been plagiarized by Edmond Rostand in *Cyrano de Bergerac*. Rostand's play was published in Paris the year after Gross copyrighted his. Gross sued and succeeded in enjoining the performance of Rostand's play in Chicago after its New York opening.

Gross divorced his wife Emily in 1909 to marry an 18-year-old girl. After the collapse of his real-estate business, he moved to Michigan with his young wife and died in 1913. The previous year Emily Gross had sold her Lake Shore Drive house, but it was taken down in 1913 to make way for the 13-story Stewart Apartments (1200 North Lake Shore Drive), designed by architect Benjamin Marshall of Marshall & Fox.

POTTER PALMER MANSION
1350 LAKE SHORE DRIVE
COBB & FROST, 1884

VIEW FROM CORNER OF LAKE SHORE DRIVE AND SCHILLER STREET

EXTERIOR SHOWING CONSERVATORY

CHICAGOANS CALLED IT "the Castle." The house Potter Palmer built on North Lake Shore Drive, in size and lavishness, rivaled the great mansions of New York City. Architect and historian Thomas Tallmadge wrote in his book *Architecture in Old Chicago*, published in 1941 after his death, "By far the most famous, probably the largest and by all odds, the most imposing house in our city is the Potter Palmer mansion, a mansion to end all mansions." It was the only Chicago house to be included in George Sheldon's influential 1886 book *Artistic Country Seats.*

Sheldon wrote, "It would be difficult to exaggerate the costliness and beauty of the finish of the principal apartments in Mr. Palmer's house; suffice it to say that few houses in any land can equal it in these respects." According to Sheldon, H. H. Richardson, who was building the MacVeagh house immediately to the north, visited the Palmer house. He admired the carved woodwork and pronounced the mosaic floor in the entry hall the handsomest floor in the country. It was perhaps the kindest thing Richardson could find to say about the enormous, somewhat awkward, medieval confection.

MAIN HALL

STAIR LANDING

LIBRARY

Potter Palmer, more than any other man of his generation, influenced the physical form and the development of the city of Chicago. Born in upstate New York in 1826, Palmer left home at the age of 18 to go into business. He opened dry-goods stores in Oneida and Lockport, New York, then sold them in 1852 when he moved to Chicago and opened P. Palmer & Company, also a dry-goods establishment. A shrewd merchant, Palmer bought in volume when wholesale prices collapsed after the financial panic of 1857. In 1860, when war with the South seemed immi-nent, he bought raw cotton and cotton goods; when cotton supplies from the South were cut off, he made a fortune.

Palmer's ability to anticipate markets and trends was a talent he applied to real estate by buying low-priced land in large parcels and then improving it with high-profile buildings. Palmer was responsible for the development of State Street, where he owned almost a mile of frontage. In 1865, he sold a controlling interest in his multi-million-dollar dry-goods business to Marshall Field and Levi Leiter. He then built a six-story, marble-clad department store on State Street with Field and Leiter, as well as Chicago's fanciest hotel,

LIBRARY FIREPLACE DETAIL

the Palmer House. When the great fire of 1871 destroyed the first Palmer House Hotel, Palmer immediately rebuilt it on an even grander scale.

At age 44, Palmer retired from his successful career, preferring the life of a playboy and big spender. He spent time in Europe and returned to Chicago as a fashionably dressed millionaire bachelor. He soon fell in love with Bertha Honore, the 21-year-old daughter of Henry Hamilton Honore, a member of Chicago's aristocratic colony of Kentuckians. Bertha and Potter were married in 1870, and the charismatic Bertha soon became the unchallenged queen of Chicago society.

As Potter Palmer helped rebuild Chicago following the fire, his glamorous wife established herself as an outspoken advocate of greater education for women, lecturing on subjects ranging from art to politics. Chicagoans were far more interested, however, in her stately carriage, her fabulous parties, and her sparkling jewels.

In 1881, Palmer began construction of Chicago's most imposing house, a castle, on Lake Shore Drive. At the time, most of Chicago's prominent families lived on Chicago's south side: on Prairie Avenue or on South Michigan Avenue. Bertha's family house was then located on South

PARLOR

Michigan Avenue, in an area known as "Millionaires' Row." Rather than build there, Palmer looked for property he could develop in addition to establishing his own residence. He bought half a mile of undeveloped lakefront property north of the center of Chicago and quickly expanded his holdings by acquiring additional property to the north, south, and west.

Palmer hired Henry Ives Cobb and Charles Sumner Frost to design his own house. Budgeted at $90,000, the residence cost more than a million dollars and took three years to build. Beautifully sited with the porte cochere facing the corner of Schiller and Lake Shore Drive, Cobb & Frost's plan opened all the major ground-floor rooms off a central two-story reception and stair hall. Palmer was unhappy with the house's exterior, although the architects claimed that Palmer had made many of the design decisions himself, as he had done at the Palmer House Hotel. When Palmer later decided to add an art gallery to display his growing collection, he hired Henry Hardenberg, the architect of New York's Plaza Hotel.

Herter & Company of New York was responsible for the original opulent decoration of the principal ground-floor rooms. R. W. Bates of

PARLOR AS REMODELED BY DAVID ADLER, 1921

Chicago designed Bertha's Moorish-style bed-room on the second floor, with ebony woodwork and gold trim. Like many houses of the era, the rooms functioned to display the Palmers' growing collections of painting, sculpture, and art objects. Each room was a decorative world unto itself, drawing on Renaissance, Gothic, Moorish, and even Eastlake motifs.

During the years the Palmers' house was under construction, members of Chicago society fol-lowed their unchallenged leaders, purchasing land from Potter Palmer. They moved en masse to Lake Shore Drive and the Astor Street area, largely abandoning the south side. Land values quadru-pled along Lake Shore Drive, originally called Palmer Boulevard, as Potter Palmer succeeded in transforming the lakefront's windswept sand dunes into Chicago's most posh address.

The Palmers' existence was governed by for-mality. Potter Palmer constructed their house without doorknobs or outside locks so that it was possible to enter only when admitted by a ser-vant. A visitor's card passed through legions of butlers, maids, and social secretaries. Even Bertha's closest friends had to write for an appointment. She typically appeared at her

ART GALLERY ADDITION

ART GALLERY LOOKING INTO VESTIBULE

VESTIBULE TO ART GALLERY ADDITION

formal dinners dressed in velvet and wearing a diamond tiara and a choker containing 2,268 pearls and seven huge diamonds. Surrounded by her collection of Monets, Degas, and Corots, she held court. Bertha Palmer was an early collector of French Impressionist painters, and her artwork formed the nucleus of the Art Institute of Chicago's Impressionist collection. When the 1893 Columbian Exposition was planned, Mrs. Palmer was appointed to chair its Board of Lady Managers. In that role, she recruited women from every state to serve with her and traveled abroad to convince European noble families to lend precious heirlooms to the fair. She also championed

an exhibition of museum-quality paintings and sculpture, including pieces from her own recently acquired Impressionist collection, at the fair's Palace of Fine Arts. She provided a venue for millions of people to see modern art, avant-garde at the time, in person.

Potter Palmer died in 1902, but Bertha continued to live in "the castle" and carried on his business dealings. When she died in 1918, she left an estate of $16 million. The house stood unoccupied from her death until 1921, when Potter Palmer Jr. and his family moved in, hiring David Adler to make alterations. By this time, many of the great houses on Lake Shore Drive had come down to

BERTHA PALMER

make way for 10- to 12-story luxury apartment buildings. In 1928, Potter Palmer Jr. sold the mansion to Vincent Bendix, head of the Bendix Aviation Corporation, for $3 million, and then Palmer Jr. bought it back from Bendix in 1933. The mansion stood vacant for years but survived until 1950, when it was taken down to make way for a high-rise apartment building.

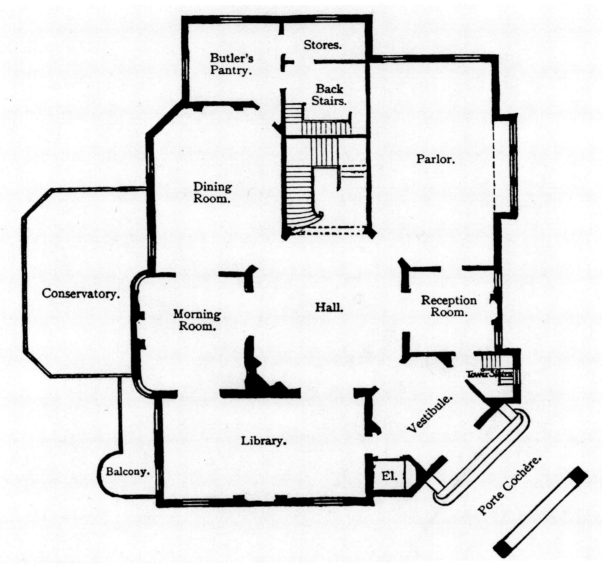

ORIGINAL FIRST FLOOR PLAN

CHICAGO ARCHBISHOP'S RESIDENCE

1550 North State Parkway

Willett & Pashley, 1885

NORTH AND WEST FACADES

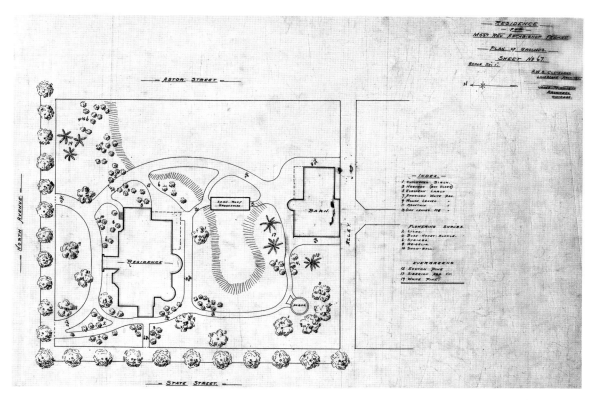

DESIGN OF GROUNDS

T HIS STATELY Queen Anne house, located just south of Lincoln Park on Chicago's Gold Coast, has served as the residence of the Archbishop of Chicago since its completion in 1885. Unlike all other 19th-century Chicago houses, it has seen few architectural modifications and no change in use or ownership. There is arguably no residence in the city that has an older, richer, and more significant story to tell. It provides a unique lens through which to view Chicago's history.

Chicago's association with Catholicism dates back to 1673, approximately 160 years before Chicago was incorporated as a town. In that year, Father Jacques Marquette, a French Jesuit missionary, and the French Canadian explorer Louis Joliet arrived at the intersection of the Des Plaines and Chicago rivers in search of a link to the Mississippi River. They were the first Europeans to arrive at the marshy southern shore of Lake Michigan.

Prominent citizens petitioned for the first church and resident pastor in 1833. Recognizing Chicago's potential as a growing population center, the Fifth Provincial Council of Baltimore recommended to the Holy See the establishment of the Diocese of Chicago in 1843. In 1844, William J. Quarter, an Irish-born priest, was sent to Chicago to serve as its first bishop. In building his fledgling diocese, one of his first property purchases consisted of 17 acres on the edge of the lake, north of the Chicago River, and cost $853. Upon Bishop Quarter's death, his brother, Father Walter Quarter, who served as administrator for the diocese, sold the land for $100 to the Mercy Sisters, who intended to open schools. Nevertheless, nothing was ever built on the property. The diocese regained ownership of the land when Bishop

WESTERN ELEVATION

NORTHERN ELEVATION

FOYER, PRESENT-DAY VIEW

Anthony O'Regan bought the land in 1856 from the Mercy Sisters for $1 and a parcel of land in Kinzie's Addition to Chicago.

Retaining the land acquired by the Church in 1844 was a clever and important move. After James Duggan, a brilliant leader who became bishop in 1862, succumbed to mental illness and in 1869 was institutionalized outside St. Louis, Bishop Thomas Foley, bishop-administrator of the diocese in Duggan's absence, used the land as collateral for loans. The size of the property expanded during this time, when Bishop Foley invited the City to dump hundreds of tons of debris from the 1871 fire into Lake Michigan, adjacent to Church property. The diocese was, because of its vast holdings, able to borrow on the land to fund the growth

of the Church. After serving the diocese selflessly for a decade of tremendous growth, Bishop Foley died in 1879.

On September 10, 1880, as Chicago's population swelled to over 500,000 people, Pope Leo XIII elevated the Diocese of Chicago to the rank of an archdiocese and appointed Patrick A. Feehan the city's first archbishop. Archbishop Feehan was born in County Tipperary, Ireland, and had served for 15 years as the Bishop of Nashville. Recognizing upon his arrival that Chicago was becoming the country's center of commerce, he had a portion at the north end of the Church-owned tract of land subdivided to build an official Archbishop's Residence that would reflect the new status of the Catholic Church in Chicago. He sold

LIVING ROOM, PRESENT-DAY VIEW

the Church property south of the residence and used the profits to create social-service agencies to accommodate the thousands of immigrants pouring into Chicago and to build new churches, houses for the aged, and orphanages. By the mid-1880s, the parcels that the Church sold off and the parcels that Potter Palmer sold off, just south of the Church property, were destined to become the Gold Coast, the city's premier location for wealthy Chicagoans to build elegant mansions.

Construction of the Archbishop's Residence began in the early 1880s. Its site was low and marshy and, although the archbishop spent $15,000 filling and grading the property, he was advised that the house would be so damp that he would never be able to live there. Archbishop

Feehan chose Major James R. Willett and his partner Alfred F. Pashley to design the residence and a coach house. Their selection resulted from a chance act of fate. Feehan had met Willett, who was a young Union Army engineering officer, at a St. Louis soldiers' hospital. Although neither Willett nor Pashley was Catholic, their firm was also engaged to design the reconstruction of Holy Name Cathedral, the Holy Name Female School, St. Catherine's Academy, and several other Catholic institutions. Archbishop Feehan was particularly interested in the local landscape and had gardens designed by Horace W. S. Cleveland. He also had a conservatory built on the residence property. Cleveland, in collaboration with William French (founding director of the Art Institute of

STAIRCASE, PRESENT-DAY VIEW

THRONE ROOM, PRESENT-DAY VIEW

Chicago), had designed the landscape plan for Chicago's North Shore suburb of Highland Park. In 1883, he began work on his most famous achievement, the Minneapolis Park System. Willett, who lived on West Jackson Boulevard, built houses and apartments throughout the city and was one of the organizers of the Chicago chapter of the American Institute of Architects. Pashley, a resident of Palos Park, Illinois, had saved many of the firm documents and among them were drawings for the Archbishop's Residence, which were donated by Pashley's family to the Archives of the Archdiocese of Chicago.

Today the Archbishop's Residence reflects the memories of great men and great events. World leaders, statesmen, prelates, and policemen walking their beat have all visited the residence. James Edward Quigley became Chicago's second archbishop after Feehan's death in 1902. In 1911 he met at the residence with Mother Frances Cabrini, America's first canonized saint, to discuss the building of Columbus Hospital. While he lived at the residence, Archbishop Mundelein was named the city's first cardinal. In 1927, he welcomed Eugenio Cardinal Pacelli, the future Pope Pius XII, and in 1937, president Franklin D. Roosevelt dined with Cardinal Mundelein at the residence. Years later, Albert Cardinal Meyer entertained Giovanni Cardinal Montini, who became Pope Paul VI. Pope John Paul II visited Cardinal Cody at the residence

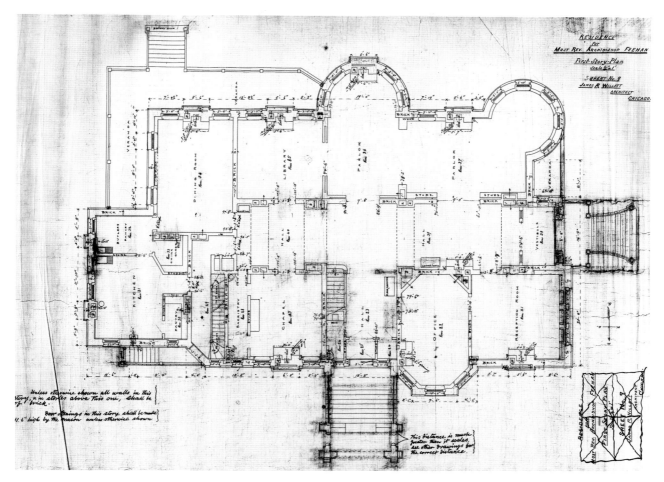

FIRST FLOOR PLAN

in 1979. The present archbishop, Francis Cardinal George, is the city's only archbishop who was born in Chicago.

The architecture of the residence is as significant as its history. Built of red brick with limestone trim, it has a picturesque silhouette, embellished with wrought ironwork and 19 highly ornamented chimneys; it is a visual delight. Noted preservation architect Walker Johnson has called it the finest example of Queen Anne architecture in Chicago. Inside, there is a great hall, parlors separated by pocket doors, and simple but elegant details including a graceful staircase, wood-paneled ceilings, and quarter-sawn oak floors. Stylistically, the carved and turned woodwork is distinctly Eastlake Victorian. The city's official Archbishop's Residence has a grand presence but the feeling of a comfortable home.

JOHN JACOB GLESSNER HOUSE
1800 SOUTH PRAIRIE AVENUE
H. H. RICHARDSON, 1885–87

LOOKING SOUTH ON PRAIRIE AVENUE FROM 18TH STREET

HENRY HOBSON RICHARDSON, who designed the Glessner house, was arguably the greatest American architect of his generation—and perhaps of the 19th century. He was an American original—pragmatic, intellectual, idiosyncratic, and a bon vivant whose friends felt he worked too hard. When they accused him of leading a monk's life, he posed for a portrait in monk's robes. Louis Sullivan observed that Richardson was like his buildings, large and robust. Richardson is credited with popularizing Romanesque Revival architecture, as these buildings are often referred to as Richardsonian Romanesque.

Popular in the 1880s and 1890s, the Richardsonian Romanesque style was significant because it allowed for a flexible, picturesque arrangement of building elements to satisfy the growing modern requirement that a building "function" by optimizing the internal arrangement of its spaces according to its use. Architecture deals with mass, surface, and space; the composition of a building's exterior masses and roof forms; the composition of window and door openings on both flat and curving surfaces; and the shaping and interconnecting of rooms and spaces. Richardson handled all these aspects with equal brilliance.

Richardson's conception of wall surfaces was unique as they were thick and capable of containing zones of space. He suggested the presence of

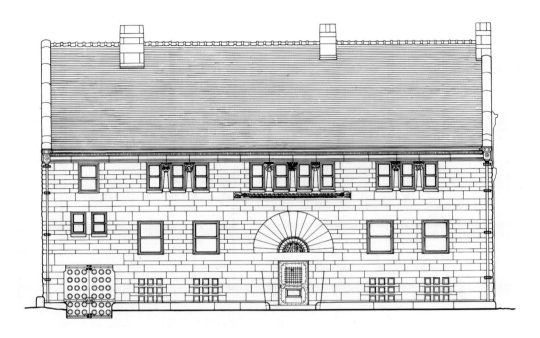

PRAIRIE AVENUE ELEVATION

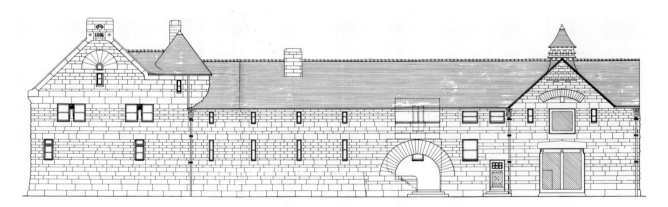

18TH STREET ELEVATION

this depth within the wall by revealing both its front and back surfaces, which can be seen at the Glessner house's arched entrance and second-floor balcony facing 18th Street. The simplicity of the Prairie Avenue facade hides a compositional masterpiece. The horizontal window alignments unify the composition, and the vertical symmetries of the openings subdivide the facade into two parts, creating strong visual centers for both the main door and the wide carriage entrance.

The planning of the Glessner house was nearly unprecedented in Chicago. The expected floor plan of a house built on a street corner would find the principal rooms arranged along the longer exterior walls, facing out. Richardson did the reverse, opening the dining room, parlor, and upstairs bedrooms

COURTYARD

to a south-facing, sunlit courtyard created by the L-shape of the building and putting the interior circulation along the 18th Street facade. Here, he expressed the first- and second-floor hallways, which required little light, by repetitive vertical slot windows that resemble those in a medieval fortification. The house's exterior stone walls are closed and private.

The Glessner house was completed after Richardson's death, but there is no question of its authorship. Richardson was educated at the Ecole des Beaux-Arts, where students were not allowed to vary their final designs from the presentation of their original sketch project (the *esquisse*). In a description of the house that John Glessner wrote many years later, he recalled that at their first dinner together in Chicago, Richardson called for a pencil and paper and said, "If you do not ask me how you get into it I will draw you a plan of your house." The sketch survives, and it matches the floor plan of the house as built. On his last visit with the Glessners, on April 6, 1886, Richardson marked places on the drawings for light fixtures, commenting, "There, Mr. Glessner, if I were to live five years longer, that is the last thing I would do on your house: my part is finished." He

FIRST FLOOR STAIR HALL

SCHOOLROOM

DINING ROOM

GLESSNERS' BEDROOM

was to live only three more weeks. Construction was supervised by his successor firm, Shepley, Rutan & Coolidge. The total cost of $74,500 did not exceed the original contract price. The Glessners moved in on December 1, 1887, and in a symbolic ceremony, they carried a burning ember from their old house on the west side of Chicago (see Portfolio, p. 293) to their new house on Prairie Avenue.

John Jacob Glessner and his wife arrived to Chicago from Ohio. After graduating from the Zanesville public schools and working for a short time in his father's newspaper office, Glessner established the firm of Warder, Bushnell & Glessner, which manufactured harvesting equip-

ment. To manage their business from a more central location, Glessner moved to Chicago. Warder moved to Washington, D.C., to handle their East Coast operation. Both hired H. H. Richardson to design their residences. In 1902, Glessner's firm merged with Deering Harvester Company and the McCormick Harvesting Machine Company to form International Harvester.

At age 42, John J. Glessner purchased three lots at the corner of 18th Street and Prairie Avenue for $50,500, with 78 feet facing Prairie Avenue and 176 feet facing 18th Street. Having acquired the property, he interviewed architects. He discussed his ideas with McKim, Mead & White and William A. Potter but hesitated to approach Richardson,

VIEW INTO GROUND FLOOR SCHOOLROOM

KITCHEN

believing the architect designed only large monu- mental buildings. Richardson responded that he would plan "anything a man wants, from a cathe- dral to a chicken coop. That's the way I make my living." Richardson had a trip planned to Chicago to meet with Marshall Field to discuss Field's wholesale store and warehouse (demolished) and stopped to visit Glessner. They went to see the Prairie Avenue site, and Richardson was hired.

The Glessners visited Richardson frequently at his Brookline, Massachusetts house, where his office was located, and the Glessners and Richardsons developed a warm relationship. Glessner particularly admired Richardson's study, which he thought was a beautiful space with "just

enough disorder to always be pleasing." In response, Richardson designed Glessner's library like his own, lined with bookshelves, with space for a large double desk and a comfortable couch facing the fireplace.

The floor plan of their 35-room house suited the Glessners' way of life. Its front entrance was located at ground level, with an inside staircase opening onto a large living hall that had doorways to the library and front parlor. The Glessners' bedroom was on the first floor, so Mr. Glessner could easily slip into his library down the hall without disturbing his wife. On the lower level, just next to the front door, was the entrance into a room where their son George, because of health

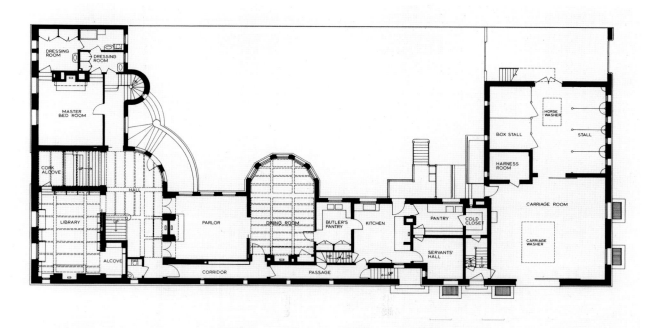

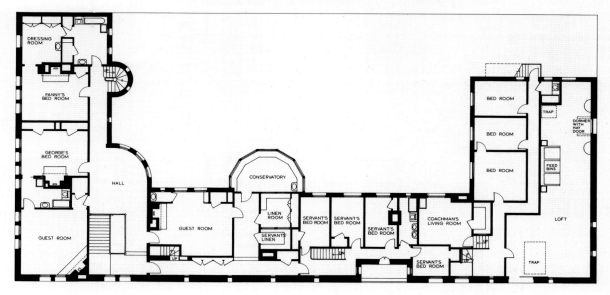

FIRST AND SECOND FLOOR PLANS

problems, was homeschooled. Upstairs were the two children's bedrooms—for George and their daughter Frances—and two guest rooms. A circular staircase accessed George's bedroom, the first-floor hall, and his ground-floor schoolroom.

John Glessner loved his new house so much that in 1923 he wrote "The Story of a House," addressed to his children. In this short essay, with its title taken from architect Viollet-le-Duc's 19th-century book of the same name, Glessner described life in their Prairie Avenue residence. He was particularly proud of Mrs. Glessner's Monday Morning Reading Club, an organization of "cultivated, congenial" women who met weekly for more than 30 years. He told how the house responded to almost any size social function, from small gatherings to musicales and drama readings for hundreds. The entire Chicago orchestra had dined there twice. Several times, Theodore Thomas brought one-third of the orchestra into the house unannounced as a surprise for Mrs. Glessner's birthday, and they played in the large second-floor living hall. The Glessners took great pride in their collection of furnishings, which included pieces by their old friend the English Arts and Crafts designer Isaac Scott; William de Morgan hand-painted tiles; dining room furniture designed by Charles Coolidge; and wallpapers, carpets, and curtains by William Morris.

When John Glessner died in 1936, four years after his wife's death, he deeded the house to the Chicago Chapter of the American Institute of Architects (AIA), wishing it to be maintained as a museum, library, gallery, and educational institution. Unable to meet his expectations because of the Depression, the AIA returned the house to Glessner's estate, and the Armour Institute of

Technology (later Illinois Institute of Technology) purchased it. In 1958, the school sold it to the Graphic Arts Technical Foundation. By this time, many of the great Prairie Avenue houses were gone or had been converted into publishing factories or rooming houses. Offices and low-rise industrial buildings were built on the empty lots.

In 1966, the Glessner house was again put on the market. It was rescued by four young men who assembled the money to purchase it. Richard Wintergreen, a draftsman in Mies van der Rohe's office, contacted his friends Paul Lurie, a lawyer; Jim Schultz, a fellow architect; and Wayne Benjamin, a municipal bond dealer, to save the house. They established the name, the Chicago School of Architecture Foundation, which is known today as the Chicago Architecture Foundation; they no longer own the Glessner house. Working with architects Harry and Ben Weese to raise $35,000, they received donations from Phyllis Lambert; C. F. Murphy Associates; Perkins & Will; Alfred Shaw & Associates; Skidmore, Owings & Merrill; Harry Weese & Associates; and Philip Johnson. Volunteers removed fluorescent lighting and laboratory sinks, keeping warm by burning the debris in the fireplaces. In 1970, the Glessner house became Chicago's first officially designated landmark and then was also designated a National Historic Landmark in 1974.

Today, the John J. Glessner House is a house museum, open to the public for tours. As a result of having received more than 6,000 objects, most from the Glessner family, the Glessner House Museum is a premier place for the study of the Arts and Crafts movement, as well as for experiencing Richardson's only remaining Chicago structure.

MRS. GLESSNER'S MONDAY MORNING READING CLUB

EDWARD E. AYER HOUSE

2 East Banks Street

BURNHAM & ROOT, 1885

CORNER OF BANKS STREET AND NORTH STATE PARKWAY

MAIN HALL AND STAIRCASE

In his essay "The City House in the West," written for *Scribner's* magazine, John Wellborn Root, Edward Ayer's architect, wrote, "Between the character of the occupant and the general expression of the dwelling there is much greater similarity than in any other part of the country." Root was probably being somewhat disingenuous toward both the role of his clients and the influence of East Coast architecture. What houses looked like usually had more to do with current architectural ideas and fashions than with their clients' personalities, but Edward Ayer was actively involved in the design of his house. He insisted that the granite fieldstones used for its exterior come from his hometown of Harvard, Illinois. The woodwork in his library was of redwood from California, where he had served in the army. Fireplace mantels were made of petrified wood from Arizona, where he later owned a mill that supplied railroad ties for the Santa Fe railroad. Ayer owned large parcels of land in Arizona and Mexico and selected Mexican onyx for the face of his dining-room fireplace.

John Root was a great admirer of Boston architect H. H. Richardson. Richardson, whose work had a huge impact on the profession, was building a house for John J. Glessner in Chicago while Root worked on the Ayers' residence. In the Ayer house

DINING ROOM

we can see Root's exploration of Richardsonian themes. For example, at the main entry, an exterior stair ascended into the recess of an arched entry porch, much like the entry at Richardson's Trinity Church Rectory in Boston or the side entrance of the Glessner house. The Ayer house's round corner tower makes a transition between the front and side facades that maintains the primary importance of the entrance, unlike Root's William Hale house (1886; see Portfolio, p. 295), where the gable-ended front and side facades are given equal importance by the corner tower. In the interior of the Ayer house, Root created architecture on a par with Richardson's. The intermediate landing in the stair hall becomes a balcony overlook brilliantly and unexpectedly positioned directly over the hearth opening, where the solid wall of the chimney flue should be. In the dining room, the obligatory wood-beamed ceiling was transformed into rows of brackets defining the space at the center of the room where the dining room table was typically located.

Edward Everett Ayer was born at Kenosha, Wisconsin in 1841 and attended the Kenosha public schools. He then lived in Harvard, Illinois, a town founded by his father. In 1860 Ayer went first to Nevada and then to California, where he enlisted in the U.S. Army. He served in the First California Calvary in California, Arizona, and New Mexico, in campaigns against the Navajo and Apache Indian tribes. He resigned his commission at Fort Craig, New Mexico, in 1864. After his military service, Ayer remained in the Southwest to purchase and run a lumber mill in Flagstaff, Arizona. He established a thriving business supplying wood railroad ties for the transcontinental

EDWARD AYER IN HIS "INDIAN ROOM"

railroads. He later moved to Chicago and founded and ran the Ayer & Lord Tie Company.

In *The Life of Edward E. Ayer* (1929), author Francis Cummins Lockwood wrote, "Mr. Ayer's early experience with the wild Indians of the West developed a study and interest in the American Aborigines. About 1880 he began the systematic collection of articles characteristic of the arts of the wild tribes." Ayer was one of the first to seriously study the culture of Native Americans. The lowest level of the circular corner tower of Ayer's house contained his "Indian Room," which held his collection of Native American artifacts—rugs, baskets, headdresses, and weapons—as well as his collection of rare books. According to Lockwood, the Indian Room was Ayer's favorite place "to sit of an evening with his wife near him, while he pored over the catalogues from foreign book sellers . . . more and more

he loved this quiet, restful room especially on a winter night when logs cut from his Lake Geneva woodland burned cheerfully in the fireplace under the mantel piece set with slabs of petrified wood, reminders of his adventurous exploits in Arizona." From 1893 to 1898, Ayer served as president of the Field Museum, which now houses his collection of Native American artifacts. Ayer also served as a director of the Newberry Library and in 1911, he donated his book collection of approximately 14,000 volumes to that institution. His bequest included many rare books on Native Americans and the exploration of the West.

In 1900, the Ayer house was sold to Henry L. Gloss. It was later subdivided into small apartments and was demolished in 1965.

FRANKLIN MacVEAGH HOUSE
103 North Lake Shore Drive
H. H. Richardson, 1886–87

FRONT ENTRANCE

CORNER OF SCHILLER STREET AND LAKE SHORE DRIVE

ARCHITECT H. H. RICHARDSON's house for Franklin and Emily MacVeagh was one of four buildings he designed in Chicago. However, Richardson was not the MacVeaghs' original architect. They began with John Wellborn Root, who designed a house for property they owned on North Michigan Avenue (then Pine Street) at Erie Street. Dissatisfied with Root's proposal, they hired New York architect William A. Potter to prepare plans. Still unhappy, MacVeagh, along with John J. Glessner, who was also planning to build, decided to approach H. H. Richardson on one of his visits to Chicago to confer with his commercial client Marshall Field. Richardson took the com-

mission in 1885 and began making plans for the MacVeaghs' Michigan Avenue property.

MacVeagh cabled Richardson to stop work when he purchased a new site from Potter Palmer just north of where Palmer was building his own residence. They began again, making new plans for a house facing the lake. Although MacVeagh signed all the correspondence with Richardson regarding the structure's design, his wife, Emily MacVeagh, was the driving force behind the project. She taught herself to draw floor plans, which she sketched out on graph paper to better communicate her wishes. Franklin MacVeagh acted as the general contractor during construction, and the

SCHILLER STREET FACADE

house was completed the following year, after Richardson's death, with the firm Shepley, Rutan, & Coolidge taking over the commission.

Franklin MacVeagh was born in 1837 in Chester County, Pennsylvania. He graduated from Yale University in 1862 and received a law degree from Columbia University in 1864. He was admitted to the New York bar that same year and practiced law in New York City from 1864 to 1866. In 1866 he moved to Chicago and went into the wholesale grocery business, and by 1874, he had

become a grocery tycoon. MacVeagh's numerous civic activities included serving as president of the Chicago Citizens' Association. In 1885, he was president of the Commercial Club and was later instrumental in getting that organization to commission Daniel Burnham to prepare his now-famous 1909 Plan of Chicago. In 1894, MacVeagh was the Democratic nominee for the U.S. Senate. He lost, and he later became a Republican. He was a founder of the Civic Reform League of Chicago and served for 29 years as a director of the

DINING ROOM

Commercial National Bank of Chicago. In 1909, President William Howard Taft nominated him as the 45th Secretary of the Treasury, a post MacVeagh held from 1909 to 1913. Although he didn't address currency reform, he did streamline the Treasury Department, eliminating more than 400 jobs. He also modernized the customs services by introducing the use of automatic electric weighing devices and allowing certified checks instead of currency in payment of custom duties. MacVeagh also oversaw the design of the buffalo nickel. At the end of Taft's term, MacVeagh returned to Chicago and his highly successful grocery business.

Emily MacVeagh was also active in civic affairs as the founder of the Municipal Art League in Chicago, a member of the Art Institute of Chicago, and a patron of *Poetry Magazine*.

The house Richardson designed was less than adequate for lavish entertaining, and, in 1892, the MacVeaghs hired Shepley, Rutan, & Coolidge to create a room on the unfinished third floor

LIBRARY

suitable for musicales and balls. The music room was designed in the French Renaissance style with gold and white ornament. Russell Sturgis, in his 1896 monograph on Richardson's successors, included it as an example of the firm's interior work. Although Sturgis complained of the lack of figurative ornament, he wrote, "But for a room designed entirely in meaningless flat patterns, this is a room of extraordinary beauty and surprising dignity of effect." In 1906, Shepley, Rutan &

Coolidge were called on again to continue to make the house more suitable for large-scale entertaining. An elevator was added to take guests directly to the grand third-floor music room, and the dining room was enlarged to the south into the existing courtyard space. Mrs. MacVeagh, the *Chicago Tribune* reported, was determined to have the largest dining room in Chicago. Here she would hold what she referred to as her "Paolo Veronese dinners," a reference to Veronese's painting *Feast*

LIBRARY, INGLENOOK, AND READING NOOK

in the House of Levi, with its architectural framework of three arches. For her grand dinners, Emily MacVeagh had tables set in the dining room, the conservatory, and à la Veronese, in the actual space between Richardson's three Romanesque arches. The dining room, along with the other ground-floor rooms, had been decorated by William Prettyman, but it was Mrs. MacVeagh's idea to pick up on Richardson's Romanesque interior details by hanging medieval tapestries on the

dining-room walls. These tapestries are currently displayed in the MacVeaghs' Washington, D.C. house, now the Mexican Cultural Institute.

Franklin MacVeagh's library was another principal ground-floor room, distinctly Richardsonian with its beamed ceiling and oak paneling. MacVeagh had been a member of the Chicago Literary Club since the 1870s, presenting nine papers to members and serving as president in 1906–7. The library was designed to accommodate

THIRD FLOOR BALLROOM

BALLROOM FIREPLACE

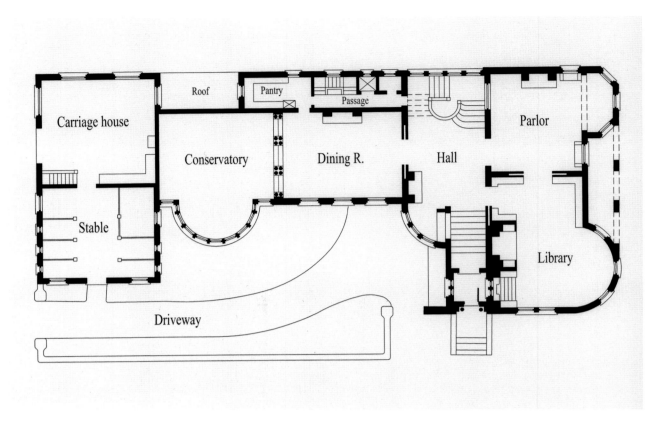

FIRST FLOOR PLAN

MacVeagh's collection of books and featured a large bay window for his desk, as well as a fireplace nook and a reading alcove that rose five steps, had a built-in sofa, and extended over the Schiller Court entry vestibule, allowing it to have west-facing windows. According to Chicago historian Mary Alice Molloy, in the MacVeagh–Richardson correspondence, Emily requested the reading nook. It was based on a photograph she had seen of a raised divan in the Kensington, London house of artist Lord Frederic Leighton.

Richardson planned the house with the main entrance opening onto Schiller, a quiet side street. A courtyard was formed on the south between the building and a high stone wall along Schiller to provide privacy for the south-facing dining room and conservatory. Facing Lake Shore Drive were a parlor and the library, offering lake views through

large east-facing windows, and a recessed porch cut into the compact volume of the principal facade. In addition to views, these features offered places to catch lake breezes in the hot, humid summertime. The battered, sloping ground-floor walls, the rock-faced coursed ashlar, the tile roof, and the shallowly recessed arched entryway were all signature features of Richardson's late work. Henry Russell Hitchcock, in his 1936 biography of Richardson, found fault with all of Richardson's work completed posthumously and in a backhanded compliment wrote of the MacVeagh house that "it is, of course, still superior to the Richardsonian work which was being done in Chicago at this time even by such architects as Adler and Sullivan and Burnham and Root, but that is saying very little." Hitchcock misses the brilliance of Richardson's Lake Shore Drive facade, a stone screen wall stretched between the polygonal bay of the parlor at the north end and the semicircular bay of the library, at the south, which turns the corner onto Schiller. A peaked roof at the north end of the house defines the edge of the building as it meets the adjacent S. E. Barrett residence. The visual suppression of these two bays into the compact mass of the building, the creation of a unified stone skin that contains both the porches, as well as the enclosed volume of the house, is uniquely Richardsonian in conception.

The MacVeagh house was demolished in 1922 to make way for an apartment building. In 1931, the Depression forced Franklin MacVeagh to liquidate his 65-year-old wholesale grocery business. He died in 1934.

MRS. JOHN C. (LYDIA) COONLEY HOUSE
1150 LAKE SHORE DRIVE
POND & POND, 1891

VIEW FROM LAKE SHORE DRIVE

LIVING ROOM

When Lydia Coonley's friend Jane Addams established Hull-House in 1889, to provide social services, education, and vocational training for the poor, the architects were Pond & Pond. Mrs. Coonley hired them to design her new Lake Shore Drive house.

Pond & Pond designed a remarkable residence for Mrs. Coonley. It was built in 1891, the same year as Louis Sullivan's Charnley house, which was only a block away, and predates by two years Frank Lloyd Wright's Winslow house, built in the suburb of River Forest. It makes an interesting comparison to both of these significant structures. The three houses all have a similar exterior ground-floor treatment and similar entryways. The Coonley house and the Winslow house both have decorative patterned brickwork or patterned terra-cotta that visually create a horizontal band of the top floor under a hipped roof and projecting eaves. Although Frank Lloyd Wright's debt to Louis Sullivan is clear, it is possible that the Winslow house, now heralded as groundbreaking, also owes a debt to Pond & Pond's design. The Pond brothers were friends of Wright's, and he surely would have known the house they built for Mrs. Coonley. Furthermore, Wright went on to build a house for one of her sons, Avery, in the suburb of Riverside.

STAIRCASE CONNECTING SECOND AND THIRD FLOORS

Lydia Arms Avery Coonley was the oldest child of Benjamin Avery, who owned the Avery Plow Works in Louisville, Kentucky, and Susan Look Avery, a radical abolitionist and suffragette. Lydia married John Clark Coonley, who, although trained as a lawyer, went to work in his father-in-law's plow-manufacturing business. In 1873, the Coonleys moved to Chicago, where John founded the Chicago Malleable Iron Company. In Chicago, Lydia actively supported the arts and social causes. She was a published author, poet, and songwriter. She was president of the Chicago Women's Club and an active member of the Society of Midland Authors and the Fortnightly. John Coonley died in 1882, and in 1897 she married Professor Henry Ward, an eminent geologist who taught at the

University of Chicago. Lydia financed his research expeditions to collect meteorites. These were eventually housed in the Geological Hall of the Museum of Natural History in New York as the Ward–Coonley Collection.

Henry Ward was killed in an automobile accident in 1906, and in 1911, Lydia Coonley-Ward sold her house and moved to the Avery family estate, Hillside, in Wyoming, New York. In 1921, her poetry was collected and published in three volumes: *The Melody of Life, The Melody of Love,* and *The Melody of Childhood.*

Lydia Coonley-Ward died in 1924. Her Lake Shore Drive house was taken down to make way for an apartment building.

MUSIC ROOM

FIRST FLOOR STAIR HALL

JAMES CHARNLEY HOUSE

1365 NORTH ASTOR STREET

ADLER & SULLIVAN, 1891–92

ASTOR STREET AND SCHILLER STREET FACADES

ASTOR STREET FACADE LOOKING NORTH

THE CHARNLEY RESIDENCE has long been considered one of Chicago's most architecturally important houses. Designed by Louis Sullivan and Frank Lloyd Wright together, the Charnleys' Astor Street house was unusual in many ways. The simple geometry and stripped-down, palazzolike character of the exterior, nearly devoid of specific historical forms and ornament, have given the house a prominent place in most histories of the development of 20th-century modern architecture.

Born in Philadelphia in 1844, James Charnley was one of 10 children. The Charnley family was well-to-do, and James was educated at Yale, graduating in 1865. Charnley began work in the Derby Iron and Steel Works in Derby, Connecticut, and in 1866 he moved to Chicago. There, along with two

of his brothers, he established a lumber business, Bradner, Charnley & Company. In 1872, he married Helen Douglas, whose father was president of the Illinois Central Railroad. In the following years, he owned and invested in a number of manufacturing companies and during the 1890s listed his occupation in the city directories as a "capitalist."

Before they moved to Astor Street, the Charnleys were among the earliest residents of Lake Shore Drive. They hired architects Burnham & Root to design a house for them in 1882 at the corner of Lake Shore Drive and Division Street and moved into the completed structure while Potter Palmer's mansion was still under construction several blocks to the north. The Charnleys' ample freestanding house had six chimneys, and its wraparound porch gave it a decidedly suburban

STAIR

character. Both of the Charnleys' young daughters died during the first year that the family lived in the house. Four years later, the couple sold it to real estate developer Samuel Gross. After renting for several years, they elected to build again, this time on an Astor Street lot they purchased from Potter Palmer. They had become friends with the architect Louis Sullivan and turned to him for the design of their new house. It may have been through Helen's father that the Charnleys first met Sullivan, as Sullivan's brother Albert was the general superintendent of the Illinois Central Railroad in the late 1880s. In the spring of 1890, Sullivan accompanied them to Ocean Springs, Mississippi, a modest resort community, where

they bought 21 acres of land. Sullivan purchased seven acres adjacent to the Charnley property and designed simple cottages for the Charnleys and himself. These were destroyed in 2005 by Hurricane Katrina.

The house Sullivan designed on Astor Street was extremely modest compared to the houses being built along Lake Shore Drive. The main floor contained a recessed entry vestibule flanked by two alcoves. To either side of the stair hall are small living and dining rooms. The layout and room sizes suggest that the Charnleys did not entertain on a large scale. On the second floor are two bedrooms, each with a private bath and fireplace. It is likely that the south bedroom, the larger

ENTRY VESTIBULE

MAIN HALL

of the two on this floor, was occupied by James and Helen. The smaller bedroom on the north was probably occupied by their son Douglas, who was 18 when they moved into their Astor Street house. The third-floor bedroom on the north side was probably occupied by John M. Douglas, Helen's brother, who lived with the Charnleys. The Charnleys had two servants who occupied the two small bedrooms on the south end of the third floor. Nothing is known of how the Charnleys lived in their house, as no interior photographs, letters, or diaries describing their activities survive.

Most historians have credited the design of the Charnleys' house to Frank Lloyd Wright. The source of this educated guess is twofold. First, the house's abstract geometric simplicity, low hipped roof, and restrained ornamentation are generally seen as the beginning of Wright's Prairie style house designs. Second, Wright claimed in his 1932 autobiography and in his 1949 book *Genius and the Mobocracy* that he designed the house. He wrote, "After building the great auditorium the firm did not build residences because they got in the way of larger, more important work. I had

STAIRCASE CONNECTING SECOND AND THIRD FLOORS

taken over dwellings . . . The Charnley house was done in this way." Wright tells us that he made the quarter-inch drawings of the Charnley house at home, probably as a way to pay off a personal loan from Sullivan that enabled him to build his own house in Oak Park. However, recent scholarship by Richard Longstreth among others, does not accept Wright's claim as proof that he in fact was the principal designer.

According to architectural historian Paul Sprague, the geometric simplification seen in the exterior of the Charnley house was typical of the work Sullivan was doing between 1887 and 1890. Further, all of the so-called bootleg houses designed by Wright during this period, and done in violation of his contract with Adler & Sullivan, have asymmetrical plans and picturesque exteriors unrelated to the formal geometry of the Charnley house. The entry facade, with its projecting second-floor balcony, is reminiscent, on a different scale, of the Auditorium Building's projecting second-floor colonnaded loggia over the Michigan Avenue entrance. Inside the Charnley house, the decorative motifs and arched openings further suggest Sullivan as the primary designer. The complete separation of the main stair from the stair hall at each level is highly unusual for houses of this period, although the stair at the main floor, where it ascends through an arched opening, is similar to the stair in Sullivan's Auditorium Building. Unprecedented in Sullivan's work, however, is the screen of wood that spindles at the side of the stair on the second floor, separating the stair run from the open space as it rises through and defines one side of a rectangular volume of space that ends at the third-floor skylight—a forerunner to the complex spaces Wright would later develop.

It is the similarities between the Charnley house and between the front entrance to Wright's Winslow house (1894) in River Forest that have made the attribution of the Charnley house design contentious. By the 1930s, historians had decided the Winslow house was important as the first of Wright's Prairie style residences. To have it appear derivative of Louis Sullivan's work would have called into question Wright's originality. Richard Longstreth, in his book *Charnley House: Louis Sullivan, Frank Lloyd Wright, and the Making of Chicago's Gold Coast*, wrote that despite the fact that Sullivan delegated some of the work in the office, "the house for James and Helen Charnley was a special case. Sullivan's close friendship with the couple, the prestigious location of their site, and the publicity the firm sought for the project all suggest that this was an important commission that would not have been simply turned over to an assistant no matter how gifted that individual."

The Charnleys lived in the house only a short time. In the late 1890s, James was diagnosed with an incurable kidney disease. He sold his Chicago company and retired in 1902 to Camden, South Carolina. The family didn't sell the house until 1911, and then it had a succession of owners. In 1986 the Skidmore, Owings & Merrill Foundation purchased the Charnley house and undertook a complete restoration of the building, including the removal of a 1926 addition that had extended south along Astor Street. This addition had moved the kitchen from its original basement location to the first floor, destroying the symmetry of Sullivan's facade. In 1994, Seymour Persky, a Chicago real-estate developer, philanthropist, and collector of architectural artifacts, leased and then purchased the house. A year later, Persky gave the house to the Society of Architectural Historians for their national headquarters. It is now known as the Charnley–Persky House and is open to the public by appointment.

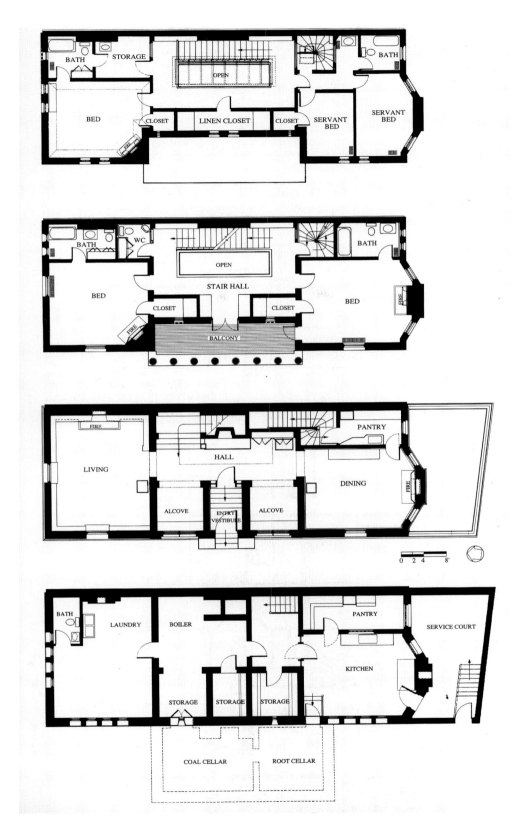

BASEMENT TO THIRD FLOOR PLANS (BOTTOM TO TOP)

WILLIAM W. KIMBALL HOUSE

1801 Prairie Avenue

Solon Beman, 1892

CORNER OF 18TH STREET AND PRAIRIE AVENUE

ENTRY PORCH DETAIL

I N 1857, William Wallace Kimball arrived in Chicago from Iowa with four pianos, which he sold to begin his business as a dealer in pianos and organs. Born in 1828 in Oxford County, Maine, Kimball worked as a store clerk, teacher, and traveling salesman before settling in Chicago. When the great fire of 1871 destroyed his showroom and offices in the Crosby Opera House on Washington Street, he quickly converted his house on South Michigan Avenue into a piano warehouse and offices. Kimball sold so many instruments that by 1882 he had opened a factory to manufacture organs and later, pianos. Kimball pianos were sold in Europe as well as America and soon gained a reputation as some of the finest instruments of their day.

In 1865, Kimball married Evalyne Cone, who became an important patron of the arts. She assembled a large art collection, which was later given to the Art Institute of Chicago.

By the 1890s, Kimball had amassed a fortune, and he purchased the property at the corner of Prairie Avenue and 18th Street from his friend George M. Pullman, the railroad sleeping-car magnate who lived on Prairie. John J. Glessner's house was located directly across from Kimball's new building site to the west. Prairie Avenue was then the home of Chicago's wealthiest and most successful entrepreneurs. Pullman had used the architect Solon Spencer Beman to build his house as well as design his company town and factory buildings.

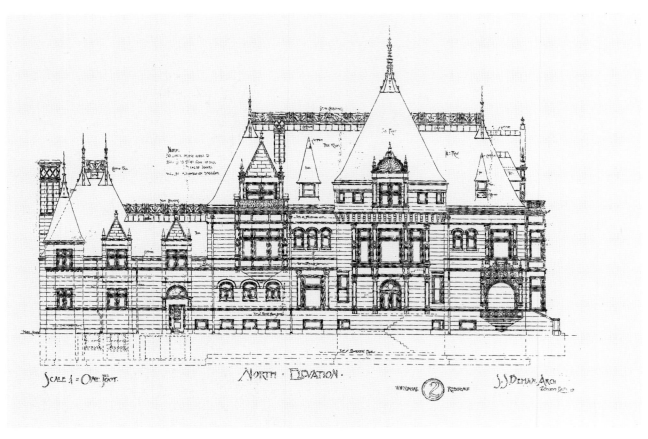

NORTH ELEVATION

So, at Pullman's recommendation, Kimball hired Beman, who designed for him a limestone-clad French château with turrets, bays, and spires. French Renaissance architecture had been popularized by Richard Morris Hunt, who had designed a French Empire-style house on Prairie Avenue for Marshall Field 10 years earlier and was the architect of a number of lavish French-style mansions in New York City. At the time, Hunt, who was the first American architect to attend the Ecole des Beaux-Arts, was considered the final word on all things French built in the United States. Beman's house for Kimball differed from Hunt's work, however, because rather than turning to Beaux-Arts sources, he modeled it after the Château de Josselin in Brittany.

Completed in 1892, it was built of tooled Bedford stone with ornate carved stone details and lavish interiors and took two years to construct at a cost of $1 million. Extending along the length of its site on 18th street, the house's north facade was made even more imposing by an attached carriage house with horse stalls and a hayloft that could be reached from the main house via the servants' back stair. Although the Glessner house also had an attached carriage house, this was an unusual feature in its day as the carriage house and later the garage were almost always located in the backyard. Akiko Busch notes in *The Geography of Home* that the garage is "a room whose appearance in the domestic floor plan was made relatively recently" and that it "holds such an esteemed position in the contemporary American floor plan" in part because of "its function as a front door and entry way."

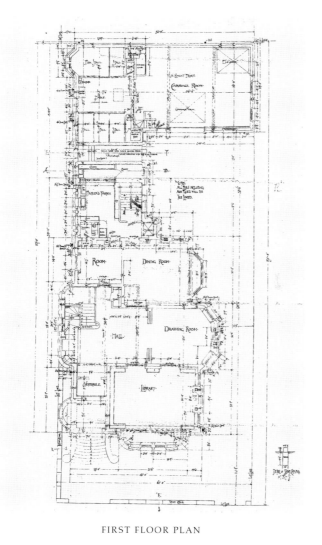

FIRST FLOOR PLAN

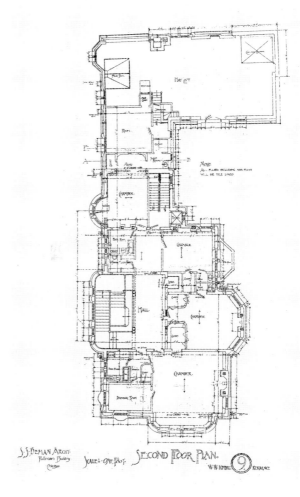

SECOND FLOOR PLAN

The house's main floor contained a grand stair hall, library, drawing room, and dining room. The interior had oak-beamed ceilings, carved wood-paneled walls, and onyx-faced fireplaces. Above the stair landing overlooking the hall was a projecting balcony, said to have contained a Kimball pipe organ designed especially for the house and manufactured in Kimball's factory.

Kimball died in 1904 and, although Prairie Avenue later fell on hard times, his château is one of the few surviving houses there. In 1924, the house was used by the Architects Club of Chicago as their headquarters. They conducted studio courses and provided living accommodations for young architectural students and during this time, a portrait of the house's architect, S. S. Beman, by Oliver Dennett Grover was prominently displayed. The Architects Club used the house up until the Great Depression, and it was later purchased by the R. R. Donnelley and Sons Company, printers, for use as office space. The house is currently occupied by the American Soccer Federation.

BRYAN LATHROP HOUSE

120 East Bellevue Place

McKim, Mead & White, 1892

BELLEVUE PLACE FACADE

ENTRY HALL, PRESENT-DAY VIEW

Architect Alfred Granger, who renovated the Bryan Lathrop house in the 1920s, called it "the most perfect piece of Georgian Architecture in Chicago." Its graceful classical details were understated and elegant. In actuality, Chicago had very few Georgian Revival houses. Built in 1892, the Lathrops' residence was an anomaly in a city where Richardsonian Romanesque dominated the design of city dwellings in the decade before the 1893 World's Columbian Exposition. After the exposition, classically inspired commercial buildings and country houses became popular, although the Georgian style never gained much popularity for residences in the city.

When the Lathrop house was under construction, the August 22, 1891, issue of the *Chicago Economist* reported, "Bryan Lathrop is building a handsome residence fronting south on Bellevue Place near the Lake Shore Drive at a cost of $40,000. Holabird and Roche are the supervising architects, the plans being prepared by McKim, Mead and White . . . It is three stories and attic high and is in the Colonial style of architecture with a decidedly Beacon Street tinge." In fact, you would expect to find this dark-red house, with its Flemish bond brick, stone trim, and curving bays, in Boston, not Chicago. The structure's austerity and dignity distinguish it from the French château next door, designed by Richard Morris Hunt in 1884 for William Borden, or the 1888 Romanesque mansion across the street, designed by Solon S. Beman and occupied by Harold and Edith Rockefeller McCormick.

The revival of colonial architecture became popular nationally immediately following the

FRONT PARLOR, PRESENT-DAY VIEW

committee and working on the Agricultural and the New York State buildings. Using a highly regarded East Coast architect had tremendous cachet, so it was understandable that McKim, Mead & White would be the Lathrops' choice. It makes equal sense that Lathrop would select the Chicago firm of Holabird & Roche to oversee his project locally. By 1890, Holabird & Roche, one of the city's top firms and well known for their Chicago School skyscrapers, had designed the Tacoma and Pontiac buildings, as well as many single-family residences. In 1889, they had designed the 12-story Caxton Building for Lathrop, designed furniture for his office, and made alterations to his house in Elmhurst, Illinois. Although he commissioned McKim for the design of his house, he remained a loyal client to Holabird & Roche, hiring them for subsequent minor changes to his new residence.

Bryan Lathrop played an important role in Chicago's real-estate community. Born in Virginia in 1844, he went to Chicago in 1865 to enter the real-estate firm of his uncle Thomas B. Bryan. One of the first tasks assigned to Lathrop was to manage Graceland Cemetery, where most of Chicago's prominent citizens are buried. Lathrop engaged Ossian C. Simonds, a Prairie-style landscape architect, to plan the world-famous garden cemetery. Simonds went to work at Graceland because he felt Bryan Lathrop was a kindred soul, as committed as he was to good landscape design.

Lathrop founded his own real-estate business and, in 1893, developed and commissioned Holabird & Roche to design the Old Colony Building, one of Chicago's few early skyscrapers still standing. He was also a charter member of the Chicago Real Estate Board. Lathrop is particularly remembered for his contributions to Chicago's cultural institutions. He served on the boards of

celebration of America's 1876 centennial celebration in Philadelphia. McKim, Mead, White, and firm member William B. Bigelow took a tour through New England to study the Georgian- and Adam- style colonial originals. Shortly after, inspired by what they saw, the firm began designing houses that became national icons. The classicism that characterized colonial architecture became the signature design feature of Chicago's 1893 World's Columbian Exposition.

The Bryan Lathrop house was designed during the years that the World's Columbian Exposition was being planned. Charles Follen McKim was in Chicago serving on the architectural planning

ENTRY HALL, PRESENT-DAY VIEW

the Art Institute, the Newberry Library, and the Chicago Symphony Orchestra, and as president of the symphony board from 1899 until his death in 1916. He was one of 10 Chicagoans who assembled the land where Orchestra Hall was built in 1904. While he served on the Lincoln Park Board, Lathrop promoted a plan to extend Lincoln Park north on landfill and is considered the person responsible for the park's expansion.

In 1875, Lathrop married Helen Lynde Aldis, the daughter of a Vermont judge. The Lathrops never had children, but Helen's widowed brother, Owen Aldis, lived with them. A leading Chicago real-estate attorney, Aldis is important in Chicago history for having developed, with Peter and Shepard Brooks of Boston, three of the city's most important Chicago School skyscrapers: the Rookery, the Monadnock Building, and the Marquette Building.

The Lathrops' house accommodated their gracious way of living and their noteworthy art collection. Helen Lathrop was a popular hostess and her annual musicales featuring grand opera stars were considered among Chicago's biggest social events. The Lathrops acquired the country's largest collection of James McNeill Whistler etchings and lithographs, which were proudly displayed in their paneled entrance hall and along the staircase.

THE FORTNIGHTLY SECOND FLOOR DINING ROOM, C. 1928

Bryan Lathrop died in 1916. Mrs. Lathrop sold their house in 1922 to the Fortnightly of Chicago, the city's first women's association. She had been a member since 1879. Founded as a literary society in 1873, it had and still has as its goal the pursuit of intellectual culture. It was founded by Kate Newell Doggett, a botanist and headmistress of a girls' school. The first paper presented was appropriately named "Culture for Women" and was given by Ellen Mitchell, the first woman to serve as a member of Chicago's Board of Education. Other distinguished members included Louise DeKoven Bowen, head of the United Charities, president of the Chicago Equal Suffrage Association and supporter of Jane Addams; Bertha Honore Palmer, chairperson of the World's Fair Board of Lady Managers; Harriet Monroe, author of a book on architect John Wellborn Root, as well as an American poet and longtime editor of *Poetry Magazine*; and Lucy Fitch Perkins, writer and illustrator of children's books. The Fortnightly attracted women with literary interests and those who were civic leaders. Their husbands were often the city's prominent civic and cultural leaders, including farm-implements magnate Cyrus McCormick, lumber baron Martin Ryerson, dry-goods merchant Charles Farwell, and Charles L. Hutchinson, who was president of the Art Institute of Chicago from 1882 to 1924.

THE FORTNIGHTLY LIVING ROOM, C. 1928

The Fortnightly of Chicago purchased the Lathrop House for $121,000 in 1922. Before then, it had met in women's residences and in several rented spaces, including the Art Institute building (then located at Van Buren Street and Michigan Avenue), the Fine Arts Building, and the ballroom of Orchestra Hall. To suit the Lathrop House to its new use, the membership remodeled and enlarged the billiard room to create an assembly space. The architect was Alfred Granger, a former student and biographer of Charles McKim. Later, a wallpaper from Zuber et Cie's historic Scenic America series was installed in a second-floor dining room, a space that had previously been Mr. Lathrop's bed-room. In 1928, Rue Winterbotham Carpenter (Mrs. John Alden) was hired to redecorate the first floor. She lightened the paneled walls of the draw-ing room, formerly Lathrop's library, added piers at the room's north end, and furnished the room with Biedermeier pieces. Her bold new interior designs for the Fortnightly were published in a 1929 issue of *Town & Country*.

Over the years, the Lathrop house changed to accommodate the Fortnightly. All work has been done with sensitivity to the elegance of the house's original design. Its simple, dignified interior remains a fine setting for Chicago women making an ongoing contribution to the arts.

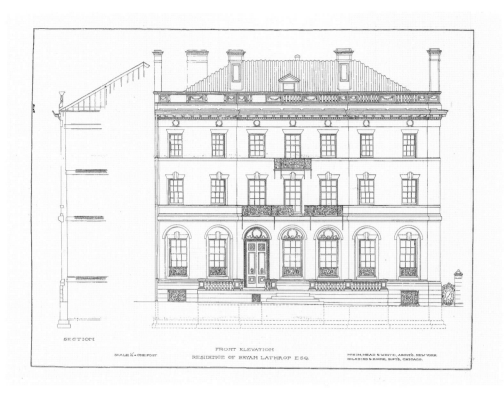

FRONT ELEVATION

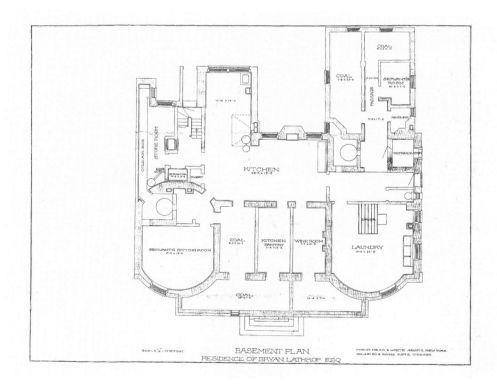

BASEMENT PLAN

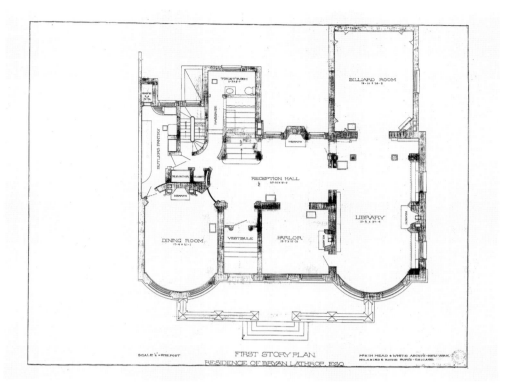

FIRST FLOOR PLAN

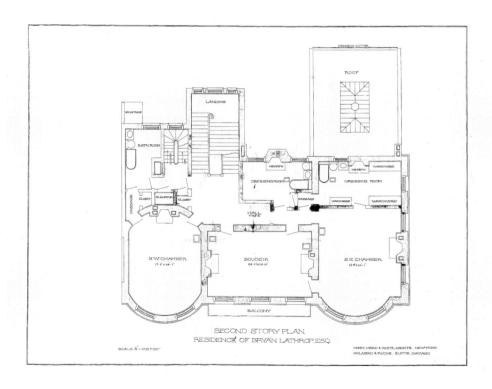

SECOND FLOOR PLAN

ROBERT WILSON PATTERSON HOUSE

1500 NORTH ASTOR STREET

McKim, Mead & White, 1892–95

BURTON STREET FACADE

ASTOR STREET FACADE WITH DAVID ADLER ADDITION

W HEN ELINOR MEDILL married Robert W. Patterson, her father, Joseph Medill, former mayor of Chicago and the publisher of the *Chicago Tribune*, hired Stanford White of McKim, Mead & White to design a house as a wedding gift. Begun in 1892 while his partner McKim was commuting to Chicago to collaborate with Daniel Burnham on the design of the World's Fair, White's design was for a four-story classical palazzo in the manner of the Italian Renaissance. The house is similar to but smaller than the house on Park Avenue in New York City White designed for J. Hampden Robb in 1889, although the proportions of the Patterson house are superior. The entry fronts of both houses have large two-story double porches supported by classical columns and topped by balustrades. The window trim is also similar, although the window groupings are not. Both houses have a clearly demarcated attic floor with small rectangular windows and a projecting cornice surmounted by a balustrade. The front facade of the Patterson house has a large central medallion on the third floor, a nod to Antonio da Sangallo's Farnese Palace in Rome. Inside, interior steps lead from the entry vestibule to a grand hall with an elegantly curving oval stair. The main living spaces were on the second floor, with bedrooms on the third and fourth. The fourth floor also contained the servants' quarters. A small service elevator and a separate dumbwaiter connected the

FRONT ELEVATION

large ground-floor kitchen to a butler's pantry on the second floor.

Robert Patterson's marriage to Elinor Medill established a publishing dynasty. Patterson, like his father-in-law, Joseph Medill, was trained as a lawyer. Patterson's father, Robert, was a prominent Chicagoan. He was the founder of Chicago's Second Presbyterian Church, where he served as pastor for 30 years before becoming president of Lake Forest College. In 1873, young Robert, choosing a career in journalism, went to work for the *Chicago Tribune.* He was successively the telegraph editor, the assistant night editor, an editorial writer, a Washington correspondent, and then managing editor. Patterson's father-in-law, Medill, had bought an interest in the *Tribune* in 1855 and served as the business manager and managing editor. It was probably Medill's support and the *Tribune*'s backing that won Abraham Lincoln his presidential nomination. During the Civil War, the *Tribune* clashed with the antiwar *Chicago Times,* which was owned by Cyrus H. McCormick. The McCormicks and Medills were reconciled by the marriage of another of Joseph Medill's daughters, Katherine, to Robert R. McCormick, Cyrus's nephew. When Joseph Medill died in 1899, his son-in-law Robert Patterson succeeded him as the *Tribune*'s editor-in-chief. When Patterson died in

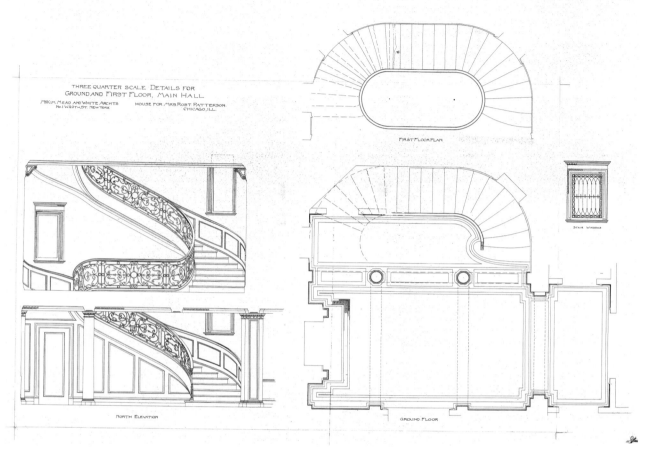

THREE QUARTER SCALE DETAILS FOR
GROUND AND FIRST FLOOR, MAIN HALL

McKim Mead and White Archts   HOUSE FOR Mrs. Robt. Patterson
No. 1 W. 20TH. ST. New York   CHICAGO, ILL.

FIRST FLOOR PLAN

STAIR WINDOWS

NORTH ELEVATION   GROUND FLOOR

DRAWING OF MAIN HALL AND STAIRCASE

1910, his son Joseph Medill Patterson became coeditor along with Robert McCormick. McCormick, who served in France in World War I was known as "the Colonel." In 1921, McCormick was one of the founders of Northwestern University's Medill School of Journalism. McCormick became the sole owner of the *Tribune* in 1925 and built a chain of newspapers in the Midwest. In 1919, Joseph Medill Patterson founded the paper that became the *New York Daily News*. Joseph's sister Eleanor "Cissy" Patterson (who changed the spelling of her name from Elinor as an adult) worked first at the *Tribune* and then at her brother's newspaper the *Daily*

News before becoming editor of Hearst's *Washington Herald*. In 1937, she leased the *Herald* and the *Washington Times* from Hearst and in the same year bought both papers from the financially ailing Hearst empire with funds from the sale of her interest in the *Chicago Tribune*. As the new owner, she merged them as the *Washington Times-Herald*. In 1940, Alicia Patterson, Joseph's daughter, also a newspaper-woman, founded *Newsday*, which the *Times Mirror* acquired in 1970.

In 1914, four years after Robert Patterson's death, the Astor Street mansion was sold to Cyrus Hall McCormick Jr., president of the McCormick

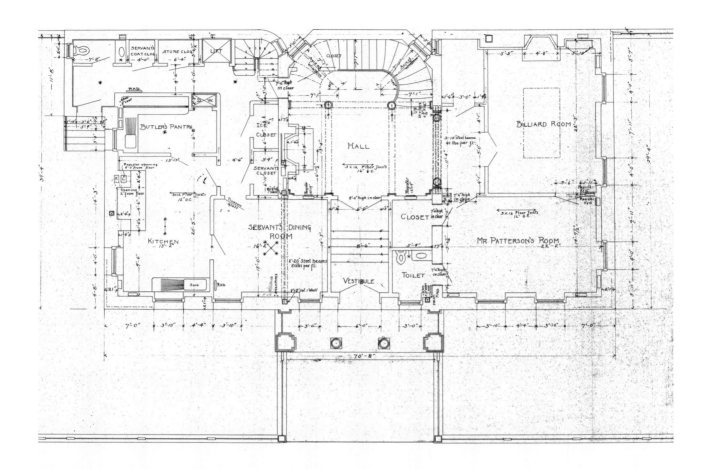

GROUND FLOOR PLAN
HOUSE FOR MRS ROBERT PATTERSON JR. CHICAGO ILL
COR ASTOR ST. AND BURTON PLACE   MS KIM MEAD AND WHITE ARCHITECTS
SCALE ¼ INCH = 1 FOOT   N° I WEST 20TH ST NEW YORK

GROUND FLOOR PLAN

Harvesting Machine Company, after his father's death in 1884. McCormick hired David Adler in 1927 to enlarge the house to the north along Astor Street. Adler matched the window spacing and exterior details, extending the house by two windows to create a new center for the east facade. Because the color of the Roman brick used for the old house could not be matched exactly, Adler's work is easily discernible, although it was designed to be seamless.

The house was used as a private school and in 1978 it was converted into nine luxury condominiums by the architectural firm of Nagle Hartray.

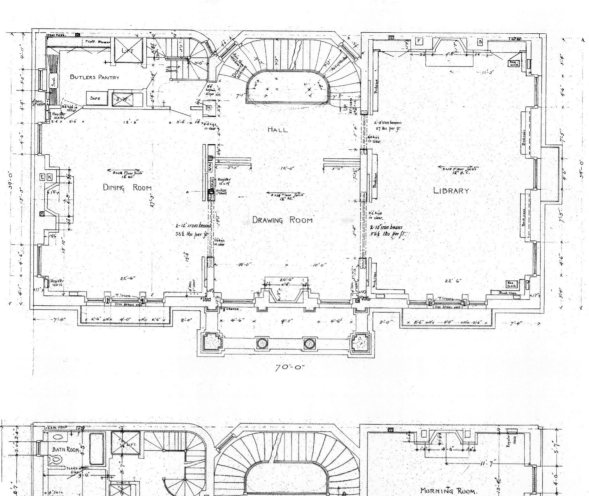

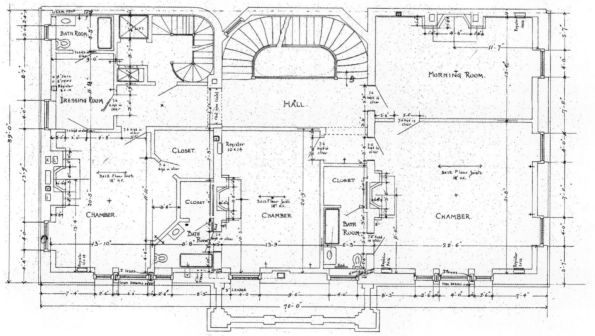

FIRST AND SECOND FLOOR PLANS

FRANCIS J. DEWES HOUSE

503 WRIGHTWOOD AVENUE

CUDELL & HERCZ, 1896

ENTRANCE DETAIL

PERSPECTIVE RENDERING BY ADOLPH CUDELL

THE FRANCIS J. DEWES HOUSE, built between 1894 and 1896, is unlike any other in Chicago. It is a confection of German Baroque and French architecture with rococo and Gothic details, combined to convey impressive opulence and the owner's financial success.

An enormously successful brewer, Dewes typified the ambitious self-made man. He was born at Losheim, Prussia in 1845, and grew up in a comfortable and respected German family. His father, a small tobacco manufacturer and brewer, was in 1848 a member of Germany's first parliament. After attending school in Cologne and learning the brewing trade from his father, Dewes spent a year in the army and, at age 23, moved to Chicago, no doubt drawn to the city by his enormous ambition and the city's economic potential. Between 1868 and 1870, he served as a bookkeeper in a Chicago brewing firm. He saved his money and acquired stock in a second brewing company, Busch &

Brand, and became its secretary and treasurer. In 1876 he married Hedwig Busch. After selling his interests in 1882, he accumulated enough money to start his own business, the F. J. Dewes Brewing Company, which he later sold to establish the Standard Brewing Company.

Dewes' financial triumph allowed him to purchase a large 45-by-70-foot corner lot on Wrightwood Avenue near Lincoln Park, a few miles north of the Gold Coast and near where another successful brewer, Joseph Theurer, was building his residence. He selected the firm of Cudell & Hercz to design two houses, one for his family and a smaller but similar house just to the west for his younger brother, August. By 1896, when he reached the age of 51, Dewes had acquired the wealth and position to commission a house comparable to city palaces in Europe, where members of the eastern European upper class led a visibly cosmopolitan way of life.

VIEW FROM WRIGHTWOOD AVENUE

HAMPDEN STREET AND WRIGHTWOOD AVENUE FACADES

ENTRY HALL LOOKING TOWARD STAIRCASE AND FOUNTAIN

MAIN STAIRCASE

LIVING ROOM

Dewes may have selected Adolph Cudell and Arthur Hercz as his architects because of their European heritage. Cudell, born in Aix-la-Chapelle, had firsthand knowledge of both French and German architecture. Dewes was no doubt impressed by the architect's fashionable clientele. In 1875, as a partner of Cudell & Blumenthal, Cudell had designed a stately French mansion on the near north side for the inventor of the reaper, Cyrus McCormick, and a large white marble palace for railroad magnate Perry H. Smith. Hercz, who was born in Hungary and studied in Vienna and Rome, had a particular interest in interior design and in theater production. He is said to have designed the interiors for 30 large churches throughout the United States and for several Chicago hotels, including the LaSalle Hotel and the Sherman House. He also produced a number of historical pageants. Hercz had originally come to Chicago to work for Daniel Burnham on the 1893 World's Columbian Exposition—itself an expression of extravagance and high drama.

Cudell & Hercz's interest in the theatrical is immediately evident on the exterior of the Dewes House. Its smooth-faced limestone facades form a basic square, but exuberant ornament drapes the angled corner bays and the front entrance and embellishes window openings. The front doorway, flanked by sculptural male and female figures supporting the balcony above, recall the caryatids of the Maiden Portal at the Erechtheum or the figures of Atlas at the New Hermitage in

DINING ROOM

St. Petersburg, Russia. But they are an anomaly in Chicago and American cities in general. The Dewes mansion combines sweeping baroque curves, intricate rococo ornament, and hints of Art Nouveau in its stone trim, delicate ironwork, and fanciful copper standing-seam roofs.

The building's exterior hints at its extraordinarily lavish interior. Its several great rooms were designed in a variety of different styles. The first floor contains four rooms and a stair hall that features gilded moldings and a niche with a wishing well and two life-size sculptures of lovers with a small figure of Cupid. The drawing room adjacent to the foyer is French rococo, with an illusionistic ceiling. It had Louis XV furniture and heavily brocaded

walls and draperies. The dining room is a mannered interpretation of classical architecture with imported French oak paneling and built-in credenzas. The Gothic library is said to have been imported from an old European castle. An enormous stained-glass window contains a door opening onto an outside balcony at the stair landing. On the third floor, Hercz designed a Louis XVI ballroom that accommodated more than 200 people. The Dewes house cost the princely sum of $200,000.

The house remained in the family until Dewes' death in 1921, when it was acquired by the Swedish Engineers Society of Chicago. They maintained it until 1973. It has recently been acquired by a private owner.

LIBRARY

SECOND FLOOR LANDING

CHAUNCEY JUSTUS BLAIR HOUSE

4830 DREXEL BOULEVARD

SHEPLEY, RUTAN & COOLIDGE, 1897

DREXEL BOULEVARD FACADE

ENTRANCE AND STAIRCASE

W HEN BANKER Chauncey Justus Blair built his fashionable south side house, he selected Boston architects Shepley, Rutan & Coolidge, the architects of the Chicago Public Library (1893), who were then at work designing a new building for the Art Institute of Chicago (1897). Shepley, Rutan & Coolidge were the successors to H. H. Richardson's practice at the time of his death in 1886 and went on to build a distinguished and successful national practice in their own names. Although they initially continued to design in the Romanesque style associated with Richardson, by the early 1890s, like many other large firms, they had turned to classicism. As their national profile grew, the firm opened offices in Chicago and St. Louis, and eventually Charles Coolidge moved to Chicago to oversee his firm's civic and residential commissions there. These included Georgian-style houses for F. S. Winston and A. Brosseau, both located on North State Parkway; remodeling work for Richardson's client Franklin MacVeagh; and the house for Chauncey and Mary Blair.

The Blairs' house was featured in *Town & Country* magazine, which referred to it as "built along rather severe lines of the Italian Renaissance period." It was a stately three-story stone and brick structure with two symmetrical curving bays and a recessed porch above the main entrance distinguished by a Palladian arch with round classical columns. The interior was composed of classically detailed rooms ranging from the Georgian-style reception room to the Napoleonic guest bedroom inspired by Percier & Fontaine. Marble Ionic columns framed either end of the entry and stair hall.

MORNING ROOM

MR. BLAIR'S DEN

GUEST ROOM

The Blairs were prominent Chicago bankers whose ancestors, traceable back to 12th-century Scotland, immigrated to America in 1718. Blair's father, Chauncey Buckley Blair, came to Chicago in 1861. Having made his fortune shipping grain to the East from Michigan City, Indiana, the senior Blair first acquired a private bank and then, in 1865, founded the Merchants' National Bank of Chicago. Chauncey Justus Blair was educated in private schools in Chicago and at the preparatory department of Racine College in Wisconsin. He began in the family banking business in 1864, and when his father died in 1899, he succeeded him. In 1903, Merchants' National Bank merged with Corn Exchange Bank, where Blair remained as a vice president until his death. He was active socially as a member of the Union League and Bankers clubs of Chicago, the Chicago Athletic Club, Onwentsia, and the Saddle & Cycle Club, among others, and he was an avid golfer

Today, the Chauncey Justus Blair house is no longer standing.

DR. GEORGE ISHAM HOUSE

1340 North State Parkway

James Gamble Rogers, 1899

NORTH STATE PARKWAY FACADE

CARRIAGE ENTRANCE

THE HOUSE THAT ARCHITECT James Gamble Rogers built for Dr. George Isham was the first and perhaps the most elaborate residence he built in Chicago. Both Rogers and Isham were graduates of Yale University. Isham was the son of socially prominent Chicago physician Dr. Ralph Isham, who was a founder of the Chicago Medical College, which became Northwestern Medical School, where he was professor of surgery and anatomy. The younger Isham studied medicine at Northwestern, graduating in 1884, and built a successful Chicago practice. He was president of both the University Club and the Chicago Geographical Society. George Isham served as a trustee of Passavant Memorial Hospital. He was also an amateur astronomer and often visited Yerkes Observatory, which was near his country house in Lake Geneva, Wisconsin. Isham was married to Katherine Porter, who was known for her administrative work for charities.

George Isham would have known Rogers socially through family connections. Rogers was married to Anne Day, whose father was the president of the Chicago Stock Exchange. The Days, who could trace their ancestors back to the *Mayflower*, were a prominent Chicago family. Anne's mother was related to the McCormicks, owners of the McCormick Reaper Works, and Anne's sister was

MAIN ENTRANCE

ENTRY HALL

HALLWAY

LIVING ROOM

married to Francis Farwell, whose father, John, started a department store with Marshall Field and had vast real-estate holdings. Francis Farwell's brother Arthur was married to George Isham's sister. Thus in addition to talent, and his education at Yale and the Ecole des Beaux-Arts, Rogers could count on his wife's family to promote his career.

The house Rogers designed for the Ishams features a prominent mansard roof and has been described as French Renaissance in style. However, James Gamble Rogers' recent biographer Aaron Betsky wrote that "the facade displays a mixture of simple classicizing window surrounds, porches, and pedimented gables, with detailing carried out in pressed brick in the 'English style' of (Richard) Norman Shaw then popular in Chicago." In fact, in his eclecticism Rogers, like the more original archi-

tects of his generation, often skillfully mixed elements instead of copying any specific precedent. Like Rogers' Lake Forest house for A. B. Dick (1902), the Isham house combines English and French motifs on both the exterior and the interior. Perhaps the most interesting exterior features of the Isham house are its modestly designed, underscaled entry porches at the house's main entrance, the carriage entrance, and the entrance to Dr. Isham's medical office, which was located on the ground floor of the south wing. These otherwise identical entrances are differentiated by the classical orders chosen for their supporting columns—Ionic columns support the office entrance porch, whereas the two entrances to the main house have Tuscan columns. The interiors are refined and classical compared to the more baroque tastes still common at the time, perhaps reflecting the influence

LIVING ROOM ALCOVE

LIBRARY

of Edith Wharton and Ogden Codman's 1897 book *The Decoration of Houses.*

Dr. Isham died in 1926. During the Depression, the mansion was subdivided into apartments, and in 1959, *Playboy* magazine publisher Hugh Hefner purchased the building. Hefner envisioned it as the ultimate bachelor pad and wrote, "Here, I knew I could throw parties equal to those held anywhere in America." He kept much of the mansion intact and added a new kitchen in the area that had been a light well, built a grotto-style swimming pool in the basement, and added a movie projection booth and hidden movie screen to the ballroom. He also had dormitory facilities constructed for the women who worked at the Playboy Club, which was located a few blocks away at 116 East Walton. This improvement was dubbed "the Bunny Hutch," because the Playboy Club's waitresses were costumed as bunnies in low-cut satin outfits and satin rabbit's ears. A brass plaque added to the front door announced in Latin, *"Si Non Oscillas, Noli Tintinnare"*—"If you don't swing, don't ring."

Hefner moved to California in 1971, and the Playboy Mansion, as it had come to be called, was donated to the School of the Art Institute. Used as student dormitories, the Isham house became known as Hefner Hall. In 1995, the house was converted to luxury condominiums. The architect for the conversion was David Seglin.

OFFICE

STAIRCASE CONNECTING SECOND AND THIRD FLOORS

ALBERT F. MADLENER HOUSE

4 WEST BURTON PLACE
SCHMIDT & GARDEN, 1901–02

BURTON STREET FACADE

COACH HOUSE AND FRONT FACADE LOOKING EAST ALONG BURTON STREET

THE STATELY HOUSE Albert Fridolin Madlener and his wife, Elsa Madlener, commissioned in 1901 on Chicago's Gold Coast is grand but in no way grandiose. The three-story structure, sheathed in warm red brick and trimmed with buff-colored Indiana limestone, at first glance appears blocklike and austere, reminiscent of an Italian palazzo. But the house's simple geometric shape is humanized with precise and elegant detailing, such as horizontal stone banding and long, narrow Roman bricks, relating it to Chicago's Prairie style tradition. Its design reflects no direct historic precedent.

Natural and geometric ornamental motifs, very much in the spirit of Louis Sullivan, are inter-

woven in the form of delicate incised stone trim around the entrance door. This design bears a striking resemblance to that of Louis Sullivan's 1892 Wainwright Tomb in St. Louis, Missouri, and to Frank Lloyd Wright's 1893 Winslow house in River Forest, Illinois.

The architects for the Madlener house were Richard Schmidt and his designer Hugh M. G. Garden. They were young architects, practicing at a time when there was considerable camaraderie among their generation of designers. Both Schmidt and Garden were active members of the Chicago Architectural Club, formed in 1895. In 1896, Schmidt was elected president. The club, whose inspirational leader and honorary member

FRONT ENTRANCE DETAIL

was Sullivan, held regular lectures and informal discussions, sponsored drawing competitions, and organized exhibitions at the Art Institute of Chicago. In addition, Schmidt and Garden participated in an informal dining club known as "the Eighteen," in which many of Chicago's most talented architects, including Robert Spencer, Dwight Perkins, Howard Van Doren Shaw, Pond & Pond, Alfred Granger, and Frank Lloyd Wright, met over lunch to talk about recent projects and debate their views. Madlener's architects no doubt assimilated and applied many of the progressive ideas being discussed, especially in their decorative treat-

ments. Garden later referred to the stone ornamental motifs and delicate bronze grillwork for the Madlener house as "Gardenesque."

The Madleners and Richard Schmidt shared not only German heritage but family ties. Albert's father moved to Chicago from Baden, Germany, in 1858 and became one of the city's leading liquor distillers and merchants. His mother, Margaretha Blatz, was the daughter of a prominent German brewer from Milwaukee. In 1898, Albert married Elsa Seipp, whose father owned beer halls throughout the city and was said to have owned Chicago's largest brewery. Elsa's oldest sister

MAIN HALL AND STAIRCASE

married Dr. Otto Schmidt, who was Richard Schmidt's younger brother. By the time he designed the Madlener house, Schmidt had already built a Chicago mansion for Joseph Theurer, who was president of the Peter Schoenhofen Brewing Company, and an office tower for Aaron Montgomery Ward's mail-order business.

Albert Madlener, who was born in 1868, entered his father's liquor business, becoming president in 1911, and afterward devoted his time to managing his own real-estate investments. When Albert and Elsa were expecting their first child, they engaged Schmidt to design their new house in the fashionable Astor Street area. They lived there with four servants and their three children, one of whom was to marry Harriet Lowden, the daughter of former governor Frank Lowden and the granddaughter of George Pullman.

Albert and Elsa Madlener developed a reputation for gracious entertaining, as had Albert's father, Fridolin, whose residence on Chicago's then-fashionable west side has been described as continuously open to friends. Like the famed John G. Glessner house, the Madleners' residence was entered at street level, with a stairway inside accessing a large living hall. This space has

LIVING ROOM

DINING ROOM

FLOOR PLANS

beautifully grained wood paneling and a fireplace with a bronze overmantel relief titled "Spirit of Waves." When the house was completed, there were no buildings on its east side, so that the music room and living room had clear views to Lake Michigan. The third floor has a grand ballroom. Although the house's interior boasts rich materials, including veined marbles, Circassian walnut, onyx, and mahogany, they are used with restraint, and an underlying geometry governs the rooms' designs.

In addition to enjoying gracious entertaining, Madlener was, like many of his contemporaries, an avid collector. He acquired coins and autographs and kept his excellent collection of Americana in a second-floor library converted from a bedroom.

Albert Madlener died in 1947. When Elsa died in 1962, Albert Jr. sold the house to a real-estate developer, and there was great public concern that the house would be demolished and replaced by a high-rise apartment building. It was subsequently sold by the developer to the Graham Foundation for Advanced Studies in the Fine Arts. The Graham Foundation, which uses the house as its headquarters, continues through grants and lectures to promote philanthropic and educational activities relating to architecture and the built environment.

FREDERIC CLAY BARTLETT HOUSE

2901 Prairie Avenue

Frost & Granger, 1902

PRAIRIE AVENUE AND 29TH STREET FACADES

PAINTING STUDIO

FREDERIC CLAY BARTLETT, an artist and art collector, was the son of millionaire Adolphus Clay Bartlett, president of Hibbard, Spencer, & Bartlett, a large, successful hardware company.

In 1902, he had a house built for himself and his wife, Dora Tripp, at 2901 Prairie Avenue, just two blocks away from the house where he grew up. Bartlett named his new residence Dorfred House, a combination of his wife's and his first names.

Bartlett commissioned architects Charles Sumner Frost and Alfred Granger to design his new Prairie Avenue house. A handsome Edwardian-style brick building, reminiscent of the work of the English architect Richard Norman Shaw, the house would have looked right at home in turn-of-the-century London. Bartlett, who by this time was

becoming known as a mural painter, designed the interiors of the house with his architects. These were worked out to display his growing collection of paintings, prints, sculptures, and curios.

The Bartlett house was arranged on three levels with a variety of ceiling heights. Steps led down into Bartlett's painting studio, which ran across the entire back of the house and measured 25 by 40 feet with a 20-foot-high ceiling. In the entry hall, Bartlett painted trompe-l'oeil shrubbery, statuary, and garden ornaments. From the ground floor, a stair from the entry hall and another from the dining room ascended to the main level, where a half-timbered Elizabethan-style hall featured framed prints of Holbein's Windsor portraits hanging on plaster panels. In the living room, Bartlett painted

ENTRY HALL

LIVING ROOM WITH VIEW TO LIBRARY (RIGHT)

LIVING ROOM

POMPEIAN ROOM

the wood-beamed ceiling with animals and swags of fruit. Alternating beams were painted with the names of famous artists and musicians. An arched opening connected the living room to a book-lined library alcove. The ground-floor dining room was painted white and incorporated Louis XVI wood paneling that he and Dora found in Europe, therefore giving it a very different sensibility from the house's other rooms.

At one end of the half-timbered hall was Bartlett's Pompeian Room, designed with a mosaic floor, wall panels painted yellow and outlined in a black and white Greek pattern, a blue ceiling with stars and the signs of the zodiac, and replicas of Pompeian bronzes on pedestals. Its designation as Pompeian describes the sculpture but doesn't fit the architecture, whose stripped-down classicism owes more to Otto Wagner's fin-de-siècle Vienna than to Roman villas. The room appears as an aesthetic non sequitur in an otherwise English-style house. Despite the open floor plan, which is in the manner of English Arts and Crafts architects, the rooms were intended as different settings for Bartlett's various activities and collections.

Bartlett was interested in the integration of painting and decoration with architecture. In 1900,

DINING ROOM

he had worked with Howard Van Doren Shaw on the remodeling of the fire-damaged Second Presbyterian Church on Michigan Avenue. This was Bartlett's first large commission, and he painted Byzantine-style murals for the church's interior. In 1905, he collaborated with Shaw again, this time painting wall decorations for the house Shaw designed for Bartlett's father at Lake Geneva, Wisconsin.

Frederic Clay Bartlett was born in 1873 in Chicago. At 18 he dropped out of school to go to Europe to study art. He was admitted to the Royal Academy in Munich and later studied in Paris with several well-known artists, including James McNeill Whistler. When he returned to Chicago, Bartlett received mural commissions and his easel paintings were soon exhibited in galleries and museums. Today, however, he is best remembered as a collector. Bartlett himself said, "I am a collector. It is a habit—a disease with me. I cannot help buying curios, antiquities, and works of art, even when I have no place to put them."

On his trips to Europe, Bartlett collected the work of important post-Impressionist and early modern artists. He later bequeathed them to the Art Institute of Chicago. Potter Palmer and Martin

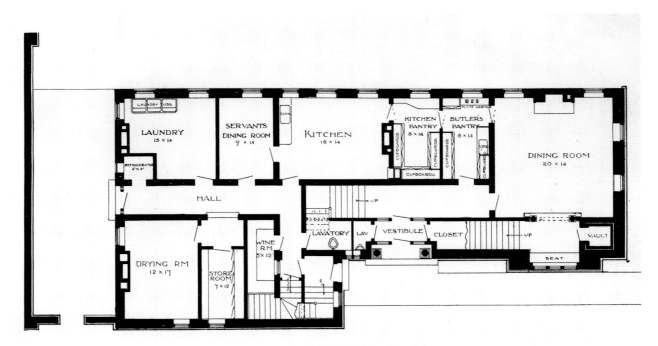

BASEMENT PLAN

AN ARTIST'S HOUSE

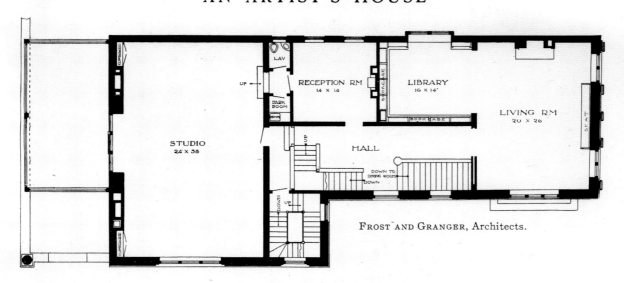

Frost and Granger, Architects.

FIRST FLOOR PLAN

FLOOR PLANS

Ryerson, who had donated their collections of Monet, Renoir, and other Impressionist painters, had founded the Art Institute, and Frederic's father had been an important supporter and a longtime trustee. In 1923, Frederic was made a trustee, and in 1926 he donated 24 paintings by Cézanne, Gauguin, van Gogh, Matisse, Picasso, and Seurat. These included Seurat's 1882 masterpiece, *A Sunday on La Grande Jatte*. The paintings were dedicated as the Helen Birch Bartlett Memorial Collection, in memory of his second wife, a poet, who died of cancer; Dora, his first wife, had died as

well. Bartlett also gave works of art to the Indianapolis Museum of Art and to the fledgling Museum of Modern Art in New York, where he was asked to be on the board of directors in 1929. Bartlett later wrote in his memoirs about the paintings he collected: "Looking back on it, it hardly seems possible that such an uproar could be created because a small group of men, banded together by a common creed who saw vibration in sunlight and blue and purple in shadows."

Today, the Frederic Clay Bartlett house is no longer standing.

JULIUS ROSENWALD HOUSE

4901 ELLIS AVENUE

NIMMONS & FELLOWS, 1903

GARDEN FACADE

VIEW FROM 49TH STREET

THE FOUNDER of *Forbes* magazine, B. C. Forbes, believed Julius Rosenwald represented the very best of American businessmen. When Rosenwald joined Sears, Roebuck & Company in 1895, sales were $750,000; they soared to more than $10 million in 1900, putting Sears ahead of Montgomery Ward, the United States' other mail-order giant. By 1914, sales had reached $100 million. But it wasn't Rosenwald's considerable business acumen that impressed Forbes; in a 1916 interview for *Leslie's Weekly*, Forbes said it was his character, "his consuming desire to help the less fortunate of his fellow creatures, be they black or white, Jews or Gentiles, young or old," that made the man. Because of his philanthropy, Rosenwald is remembered as one of the greatest men in the history of Chicago. He

amassed a fortune of over $200 million and gave away more than $50 million.

The son of German Jewish immigrants, Julius Rosenwald was born in 1862 in Springfield, Illinois, where his father ran his mother's family clothing store. JR, as he came to be called by friends, was young and ambitious, and he took jobs pumping a church organ, peddling papers, and selling pamphlets describing a monument to Abraham Lincoln when it was dedicated. At age 16, he set out for New York to clerk in his uncle's clothing store. After acquiring enough capital to start off on his own, he moved to Chicago and in 1885 joined up with his cousin to form a men's-clothing manufacturing business. Sears, Roebuck & Company, established in 1893, was one of his major customers. In 1895, when Alvah Roebuck retired and

ENTRANCE DETAIL

Sears' mail-order operation needed an infusion of capital, Rosenwald invested $37,500 and purchased a quarter interest in the company. He later purchased another quarter interest and, in 1910, when Richard Sears died, succeeded him as president.

The Sears company's phenomenal success under Rosenwald was due to his astute management philosophy. He understood that Sears' primary responsibility was to the consumer and always kept in mind the best interests of his farming clientele. He pledged to them, "Satisfaction or your money back." Success was virtually guaranteed if customers had the option of returning what they bought with no questions asked. Also,

Rosenwald figured that more people would buy if he sold honest merchandise for less money.

Rosenwald said that "the fellow at the top usually gets too much credit" and tended to attribute his success partly to luck and partly to the loyalty of his coworkers. He earned their loyalty by his actions. He set up a savings system, with the company depositing a specified amount of each employee's earnings into individual accounts. He established profit sharing and gave bonuses on the anniversary of a worker's employment. When the stock market crashed in 1929, Rosenwald, who was then chairman of Sears, Roebuck, personally guaranteed the accounts of all 40,000 employees.

STAIRCASE AND LIVING ROOM

FIREPLACE NOOK

LIVING ROOM

Rosenwald's business success was overshadowed by his philanthropy. He viewed charity as "the one pleasure that never wears out," according to his obituary. He is particularly remembered for the generous amounts of money he gave to improve the living conditions and elevate the status of black Americans. Impressed with the success of the African American educator Booker T. Washington, he donated money to the Tuskegee Institute in Alabama. Between 1913 and 1930, Rosenwald provided seed money to fund the construction of more than 5,300 schools in the rural South. His initiative led to a cooperative venture investing $20 million, including tax money, private donations, and $4 million contributed by blacks. Rosenwald also contributed to the construction of black YMCAs and YWCAs. In Chicago, he developed a model housing project for middle-class blacks, similar to the garden apartments built by John D. Rockefeller in Harlem. Rosenwald's biographer and grandson, Peter M. Ascoli, has commented that Rosenwald was most proud of his work with African Americans.

Julius Rosenwald financially supported Jewish causes, as well. He served as president of the Associated Jewish Charities and contributed time and money to the Chicago Hebrew Institute, which was devoted to meeting the needs of Eastern

DINING ROOM

European Jewish immigrants. One of his philanthropies combined two of his strongest interests—Judaism and farming. He established the Agricultural Aid Society to help Jewish farmers find work. The concept of self-help was important to Rosenwald, and many of his philanthropies directly engaged the recipients in contributing toward their own betterment.

Although Rosenwald never wanted his name attached to the buildings he funded, it is frequently associated with two of Chicago's most prominent institutions. He donated a significant amount of money to the University of Chicago, and he gave $5 million to reconstruct the Fine Arts

Building of the 1893 World's Columbian Exposition and convert it into an industrial museum. Rosenwald died in 1932, one year before the opening of Chicago's world-famous Museum of Science and Industry.

Rosenwald's house reflects his practical entrepreneurial spirit as well as his increasing wealth. Designed in 1903 by the architectural firm of Nimmons & Fellows, its flat brick wall surfaces, sparse ornament, and crisp detailing resemble the commercial and industrial architecture Chicago is known for. The "Chicago window," made up of a central fixed window flanked by two operable, narrower side windows, is a prominent feature. The

BILLIARD ROOM

horizontal band that forms the sill of the third-floor windows, together with a low-hipped roof with broad eaves, relates the design of Rosenwald's house to the Prairie School movement. Rosenwald's house was described in the July 1905 *Architectural Record* as "plain, even severe" and as dignified but without the slightest pretention. JR's house looks considerably different from the more traditional ones preferred by his Kenwood neighbors and also contrasts with the Collegiate Gothic buildings of the nearby University of Chicago. The landscape of JR's house was designed by Jens Jensen, who is best known for his Prairie style landscapes based on the Midwest's natural terrain.

Yet for Rosenwald, he designed a more traditional formal garden.

The interior is Arts and Crafts, uncomplicated and unadorned by classical or Gothic embellishments. Windows are left bare, with no draperies to obscure their shape. Geometry, not history, dominates the architectural detailing. In this respect, the inside of the house, like its exterior, reflects the progressive spirit of Frank Lloyd Wright and his colleagues. Its floor plan, however, like the rectangular shape of the house, is traditional, with the interior space divided into discreet, clearly defined rooms. It is very unlike the nearby Robie House, designed by Wright, which was to "break the box"

COACH HOUSE

with spaces that flow into each other, defying a clear distinction between rooms.

Nimmons & Fellow's reputation was based on their commercial work, much of which was commissioned by Sears; they designed few residences. Several years after the Rosenwalds moved into their new house, JR hired the firm to design the sprawling campus headquarters for Sears on the west side of Chicago.

Julius Rosenwald's house serves as a substantive reminder of the life of a great man. Most of Chicago's Sears complex has been taken down and replaced by a condominium development. Just before JR's death, his five children established the Rosenwald Family Association to perpetuate his philanthropy. Rosenwald was critical of endowments in perpetuity, and the Rosenwald endowment was spent within 25 years. Although the money is gone, Julius Rosenwald's legacy has continued well beyond his lifetime.

ERNEST J. MAGERSTADT HOUSE

4930 South Greenwood Avenue

George Maher, 1906–08

GREENWOOD AVENUE FACADE

FRONT ENTRANCE

ENTRANCE COLUMN DETAIL

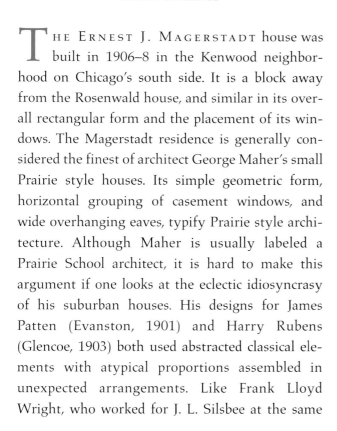

THE ERNEST J. MAGERSTADT house was built in 1906–8 in the Kenwood neighborhood on Chicago's south side. It is a block away from the Rosenwald house, and similar in its overall rectangular form and the placement of its windows. The Magerstadt residence is generally considered the finest of architect George Maher's small Prairie style houses. Its simple geometric form, horizontal grouping of casement windows, and wide overhanging eaves, typify Prairie style architecture. Although Maher is usually labeled a Prairie School architect, it is hard to make this argument if one looks at the eclectic idiosyncrasy of his suburban houses. His designs for James Patten (Evanston, 1901) and Harry Rubens (Glencoe, 1903) both used abstracted classical elements with atypical proportions assembled in unexpected arrangements. Like Frank Lloyd Wright, who worked for J. L. Silsbee at the same

time as Maher, George Maher designed art-glass windows, furniture, rugs, and lighting fixtures for his residential commissions.

Like so many of his contemporaries, George Maher was searching for an idiom that represented indigenous American architecture. He developed his interpretation through the repetition of geometric forms and decorative motifs that had the effect of unifying his designs. He called this method the "motif rhythm theory," which he described in a 1907 article, published in *Architectural Record* while the Magerstadt house was under construction and titled "A Plea for Indigenous Art." Maher wrote, "The fundamental principle being to receive the dominant interpretation from the patron, taking into strict account his needs, his temperament, and environment, influenced by local color and atmosphere in surrounding flora and nature, with these vital inspirations at

LIVING ROOM

DINING ROOM

STAIRCASE

HALL MANTEL

FIRST AND SECOND FLOOR PLANS

hand, the design naturally crystallizes and motifs appear which being consistently utilized will make each object, whether it be construction, furniture or decoration, related." Although not as eloquent as John Wellborn Root, Louis Sullivan, or Frank Lloyd Wright, Maher was describing, as they had, what is now known as an organic theory of architecture.

At the Magerstadt house, a stylized flower, the poppy, was Maher's repeated motif. It forms the capitals of the columns on the front porch and at the front entrance. It is the basis for the house's art-glass windows and appears in a painted frieze just below the vaulted ceiling in the dining room. Yet the house's most dramatic feature is the entry and stair hall, a space at the center of the house, which opens two stories vertically. Here, the main stair ascends with a stepping stair rail and balusters that form a repeating geometric pattern.

Maher's client, Ernest Magerstadt, was born in

Germany in 1864 and came to Chicago with his parents while still an infant. Educated in Chicago's public schools, he started a coal business with his brother in 1878 and operated it for 20 years. He was appointed Chicago's superintendent of streets under Mayor Hempstead Washburne. From 1894 to 1899 he was a clerk of the criminal court of Cook County, and from 1899 to 1901 he was sheriff of the county. He then served as city collector until 1911, when he went into business again. His firm, the Railway Utilities Company, supplied destination signs and other equipment for railroad and public-transportation stations. Magerstadt died in 1934, and his wife, Hattie, lived in the Greenwood Avenue house until 1957. Upon her death, their daughter Della lived there, until 1963 when it was sold to a couple who worked for the University of Chicago. The house remains a private residence today.

FREDERICK C. ROBIE HOUSE

5757 SOUTH WOODLAWN AVENUE

FRANK LLOYD WRIGHT, 1908–10

57TH STREET FACADE

57TH STREET FACADE

SCHOLARS MAY DEBATE which is Frank Lloyd Wright's most important and influential house. But aficionados agree that the Robie House is the one must-see Wright residence in Chicago, as it ranks among the most significant examples of American residential architecture. At the time it was built between 1908 and 1910, the house was unlike any in Chicago and differed radically from its Hyde Park neighbors. The drama of its Prairie style design, with sweeping horizontals and fascinating geometric detailing, was unmatched in a city of many architectural masterpieces.

Hyde Park is a residential neighborhood of large traditional houses surrounding the University of Chicago, the preeminent academic institution of the city, which was founded in 1892. Despite the liberal spirit historically associated with the university, the design of its architecture was conservative and steeped in tradition. Predominantly Collegiate Gothic, the campus's quadrangles recall Cambridge and Oxford, a remarkable contrast to Wright's progressive architectural vision.

Frederick C. Robie was born in 1879. He grew up in a traditional Victorian house, the only son of a father successful in the bicycle business. Although he attended the school of mechanical engineering at Purdue, he spent his time there selling bicycles. He never finished, returning to Chicago to work for his father. In 1902 he married Lora Hieronymus from Springfield, Illinois, where Wright had created a stunning Prairie style house for Susan Lawrence Dana in 1901–04.

Robie was young, energetic, ambitious, and beginning to share in the prosperity of his father's

FRONT ENTRANCE

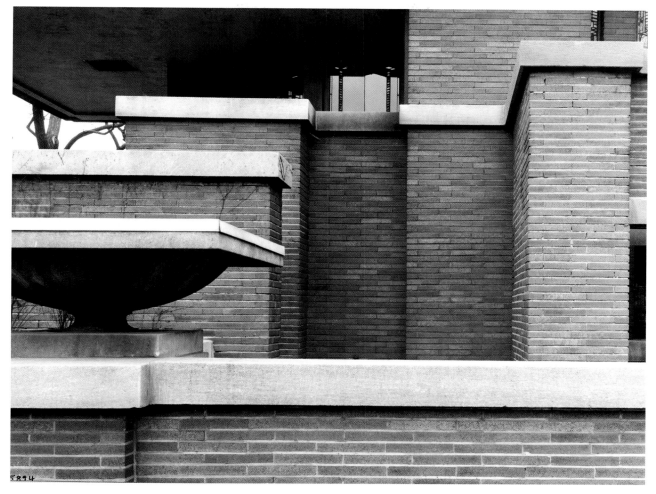

TERRACE AND URN DETAIL

business. But he dreamed of bigger things, particularly the manufacture of automobiles. Shortly before he began thinking about a house for his young family, he developed a prototype for a light car to be built by the Robie Motor Car Co., which had a store in Chicago. This endeavor never got launched. He was far more successful, however, in seeing his dream house built.

In 1908, land became available at 57th and Woodlawn, and Robie spent $13,500 for a 60-by-180-foot corner lot. He envisioned the new house carefully. He knew he didn't want it to have "box like partitions" or long hallways. He hated windows with curvatures and "doodads" and didn't want heavy drapes or bric-a-brac lying around to gather dust. He was preoccupied with light. Finally he said to himself, as reported by his son 50 years later, "Oh, I know what you want—one of those damn—one of those Wright houses." Intrigued by Wright's ideas, he figured, "Well, if he was a nut, and I was maybe, we'd get along swell." For a total of $59,000, Robie got the house he dreamed of, with furnishings specially designed by the Neidecken-Walbridge Company of Milwaukee and handwoven rugs from Austria.

When Robie built his house, the only nearby houses were on the north side of his property. The rest of the area was flat, open prairie. The Robies

FOYER AND STAIRCASE TO MAIN LEVEL

UPPER ENTRY HALL

LIVING ROOM

could be in their living room and enjoy a 1,400-foot uninterrupted view south across the Midway Plaisance, which had been the amusement midway for the 1893 World's Columbian Exposition. Today the house rests in a dense urban neighborhood.

Unlike the Rosenwald and the Magerstadt houses, which had non-traditional features, but were traditional in shape and floor plan, the Robie House was radically modern. The house wasn't a simple rectangle comprising separate rooms. Rather, it first and foremost embraced its prairie setting. Broad overhangs, sheltering rooflines, bands of leaded windows, and terraces extending from the house echoed the horizontality of

Chicago's most insistent geographic feature. Rows of slender orange-black Roman bricks, tuckpointed with continuous raked-back horizontal mortar joints and flush vertical joints that read as invisible, reinforce the horizontality of Wright's design.

Although the floor plan was designed to meet the functional needs of the Robie family, movement through the house is an experience in the unexpected. Entrance is from the west, beneath a sheltered walkway. The ground floor contains children's spaces, specifically a billiard room and a playroom opening into a protected play area set behind the upstairs terrace. Stairs lead from the ground-floor entrance foyer up to the living and

LIVING ROOM LOOKING TOWARD FIREPLACE

dining areas, which are treated as a single long space, separated by only a brick fireplace. A wall of glass doors opens onto a balcony measuring five and a half by nearly 50 feet. The third floor has three bedrooms, with the master bedroom commanding the view south.

A massive brick chimney anchors the house, shiplike in its long, floating presence, to the earth. The building has no attic and no damp basement. All service spaces, including the mechanical rooms, kitchen, guest rooms, and servants' rooms, are relegated to the north end of the lot, where a neighboring house was located. The family living areas faced the uninterrupted vista to the south and were sited to maximize light and air. To the east is an attached three-car garage—appropriate for a client whose passion was cars, but extraordinary for the year 1909.

Geometry dominates the interior as well as the exterior. Oak screens ventilate closets and hide radiators, but more importantly, they separate spaces, only hinting at the rooms located beyond. Connections are subtle. In the living room and dining rooms, bands of oak boards on the ceiling connect the custom-designed light fixtures, simple globes of light. The furniture, slatted and geometric,

DINING ROOM

reinforces Wright's characteristic architectural features. Repetition of the architecture is everywhere, from the specially woven earth-tone rugs to the exquisite leaded green, brown, and rose-tone windows with their glints of violet and turquoise. The complicated stained-glass patterns, when inspected closely, reflect the diagonal prow ends of the Robie House floor plan. The presence of Wright's hand is apparent throughout this incredible house.

Just as the house was being completed, Robie's world disintegrated. His father died, leaving him with $1 million in debts to settle. He was distraught and depressed, and his marriage ended. So did his residency in the dream house. In December 1911, Robie sold the property to David Lee Taylor, president of an advertising agency, and left everything behind but his clothes and personal effects. Only a year later Taylor died and the house was purchased by the mercantile agent Marshall Dodge Wilber and his wife, Isadora, who kept Wright and Robie's vision intact. Before Wilber sold the house and all its furnishings in 1926 to the Chicago Theological Seminary, Wright stopped over, his cape flying, and proclaimed, "This is the best example of my work."

KITCHEN

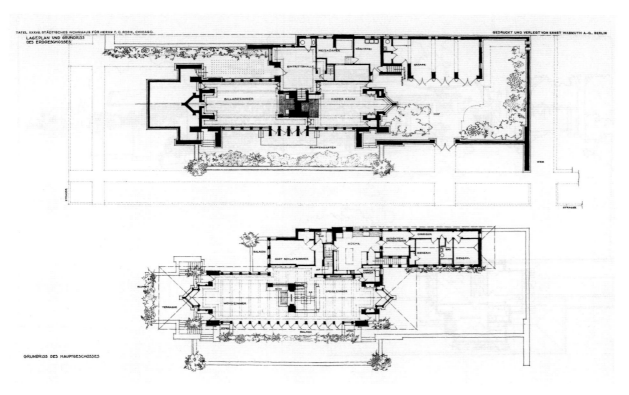

PLANS

FREDERICK C. ROBIE HOUSE

From 1926 on, the destiny of the Robie House was precarious. In 1941, the house was threatened with demolition, prevented only by a committee formed to ensure its preservation. In 1956–57, the seminary again proposed to demolish it, this time to replace it with a high-rise dormitory. When Wright visited, shortly before his death, he commented, "To destroy it would be like destroying a great piece of sculpture or a great work of art . . . it is particularly sad the professional religionists should be the executioners . . . It all goes to show the danger of entrusting anything spiritual to the clergy." A last-minute rescue came through a meeting between Mayor Richard J. Daley between Julian Levi, the president of the University of Chicago, and William Zeckendorf, whose firm, Webb & Knapp, was overseeing urban-renewal work in Hyde Park. Zeckendorf purchased the house for $125,000 and used it as his construction office until 1963, when he gave the house to the University of Chicago. The university used it for offices until it leased the house to the National Trust for Historic Preservation, which made it one of their 21 historic sites. It also later became National Historic Landmark. Currently, the Frank Lloyd Wright Preservation Trust, which also manages the Frank Lloyd Wright Home and Studio, is raising more than $8 million to restore the house and operate it as a museum. Today, the house is open to the public.

WILLIAM O. GOODMAN RESIDENCE

1355 North Astor Street

Howard Van Doren Shaw, 1911

NORTH ASTOR STREET FACADE

GROUND FLOOR ENTRY HALL

William O. Goodman, like Howard Van Doren Shaw, originally lived in Hyde Park near the University of Chicago. In 1895, Goodman built a house at 5026 Greenwood Avenue designed by Treat & Foltz. Between 1895 and 1910, Howard Shaw created nine houses on Woodlawn, the street parallel to Greenwood one block to the east. Within a block of Goodman's residence, Shaw also built another two houses on Greenwood, and therefore, Goodman could hardly have walked home from the train or taken a stroll without passing Shaw's handiwork. Like Shaw, Goodman belonged to the Cliff Dwellers Club, which was located atop Orchestra Hall in a space designed by Shaw. When Goodman decided to move to the fashionable Astor Street area, it was no surprise

that he asked Shaw to design his townhouse, which was completed in 1911.

Shaw's Hyde Park houses were all freestanding structures, more suburban in character than the party-wall houses being built on Astor Street. In his design for the Goodmans, Shaw explored what for him was a new house type: the Renaissance palazzo with a piano nobile. Built from lot line to lot line, the house is L-shaped, creating behind the street facade a south-facing courtyard accessed through a carriageway that passes under the house's south end. Along the north side of the courtyard, the ground level contains a garage, a laundry, and the boiler room. The courtyard is paved and landscaped with a fountain against its east wall serving as a terminus to the space. From Astor Street, the entry

FIRST FLOOR HALL AND STAIR TO SECOND FLOOR

SECOND FLOOR HALL

LIVING ROOM

LIBRARY

vestibule opens to a hall with a fireplace, a grand stairway that connects to the second floor, and an elevator that serves all levels of the house. On the second floor, the living room occupies the full 42-foot depth of the house, with one end overlooking the street and the other facing east over the court-yard. The remainder of the Astor Street frontage is taken up by a library and a sitting room, with the dining room located in the north wing with views over the courtyard. The living room and second-floor stair hall both have oak-beamed ceilings, and the sitting room has oak-paneled walls. In the library, the bookcases lining the walls have

unusual scalloped arched tops that give them the look of freestanding cabinets. Family bedrooms are on the third floor. Shaw's interior detailing, plasterwork, and woodwork combined motifs from both English and French architecture in often unexpected ways but, except for the entry hall, seem unrelated to the house's classical exterior.

The style of the house was also a departure for Shaw. Most of his work up to this time was English Arts and Crafts, American Colonial, Tudor, or Georgian, although the 1906 house Shaw designed for Edward Ryerson in Lake Forest, Illinois, was classical. It is interesting to note that Ecole des

SMOKING ROOM

Beaux Arts–trained David Adler was in Shaw's office from 1911 to 1912 and Adler's future partner Henry Dangler worked for Shaw from 1909 to 1912. Both men went on to design classical houses.

William Owen Goodman was born in 1848 in Wellsboro, Pennsylvania. His mother's family arrived in Pennsylvania in 1682 with William Penn. In 1866 he went to work for an uncle who was a lumber dealer in Athens, Pennsylvania, and two years later he moved to Chicago, taking a position as a bookkeeper and salesman for Spalding & Porter, who were in the lumber business. In 1878 he married Erna Sawyer, the daugh-

ter of a U.S. senator from Wisconsin. Along with his father-in-law, Philetus Sawyer, he soon began investing in lumber in Illinois, Indiana, Wisconsin, and Nebraska, forming the firm of Sawyer, Goodman & Company, later the Sawyer-Goodman Company and the Goodman Lumber Company of Wisconsin.

Goodman was a trustee of the Chicago Orchestra Association and of the Art Institute of Chicago, for which Howard Van Doren Shaw later built McClintock Court, remodeled the space that is now the Ryerson and Burnham Libraries, and designed the Goodman Theater building.

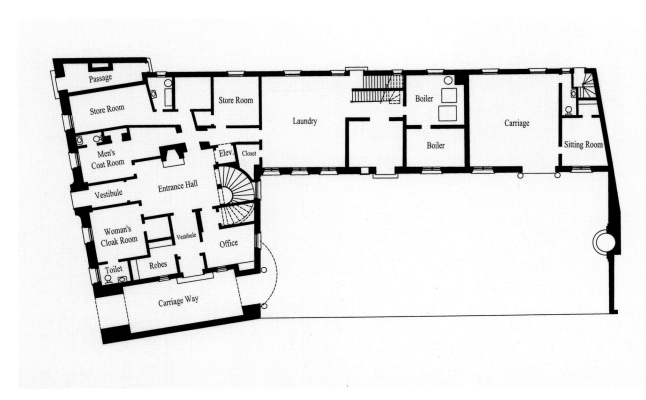

GROUND FLOOR PLAN

William and Erna Goodman had only one child, a son, Kenneth Sawyer Goodman. The young Goodman was a playwright who died in the flu epidemic of 1918 while at the Great Lakes Naval Training Station. William Goodman commissioned Shaw to design a simple neoclassical mausoleum, which was built at Graceland Cemetery as his son's tomb. He donated $300,000 to the Art Institute to construct a theater as a memorial to his son's memory and established an endowment of $150,000 to found a professional repertory company and a theater department at the School of the Art Institute. Shaw designed the theater with a one-story classical entryway and stairs down to the auditorium, which was located at a lower level to meet city height restrictions imposed to keep the structure from blocking views of the lake from Michigan Avenue. The theater

was inaugurated in October 1925 with the performance of three plays written by Kenneth Goodman: *Back of the Yards, The Green Scarf,* and *The Game of Chess.*

The Goodmans' residence has fared better than the theater they built in their son's name. Their house still stands on Astor Street just south of the Charnley house and has long been referred to as "the Court of the Golden Hand," a reference to the cast-brass knocker in the shape of a hand, mounted on the doors to the carriageway. Shaw's handsome wood-paneled theater with niches for busts of the world's great playwrights was taken down in 2005 to make way for a steel-and-glass expansion of the Art Institute's gallery space, ignoring Goodman's legacy and destroying an important work by Howard Van Doren Shaw, who was asked at one time to take over the Art Institute's directorship.

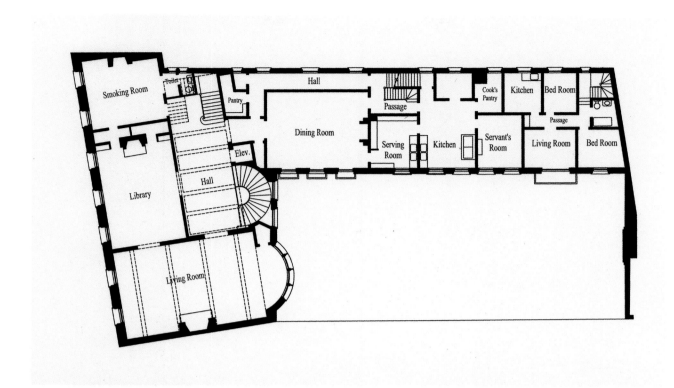

FIRST FLOOR PLAN

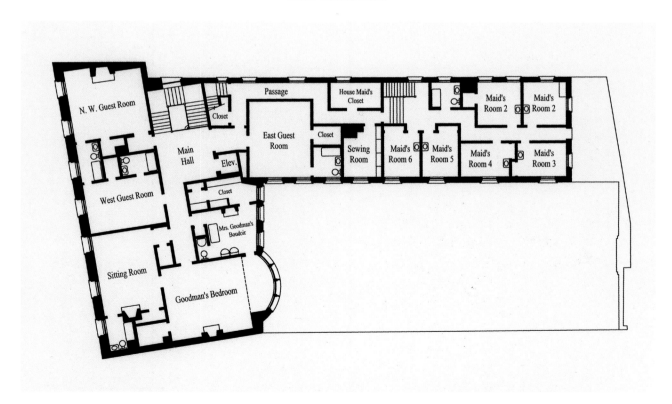

SECOND FLOOR PLAN

EDWARD MORRIS HOUSE

4800 South Drexel Boulevard

Howard Van Doren Shaw, 1913

DREXEL BOULEVARD FACADE

48TH STREET AND DREXEL BOULEVARD FACADES

T HE LARGE BRICK-AND-STONE English Tudor mansion that Howard Van Doren Shaw designed for meatpacker Edward Morris in 1913, although located in Kenwood on Chicago's south side, would look right at home in Lake Forest. However, unlike its suburban counterparts, it was built very close to the street. The house, situated on a large piece of property, boasted a huge coach house and servants' quarters with a cupola and attached greenhouse. The gardens were designed by Rose Standish Nichols, the distinguished Boston landscape architect, author, and prominent suffragette, who had collaborated with Shaw in 1908 on the gardens for the Hugh

McBirney house in Lake Forest. Morris' grounds included a kitchen garden, flower gardens, and a Tudor-style tea house designed by Shaw, as well as a garden pergola and a tennis court. By 1913, Shaw no longer lived in the Hyde Park–Kenwood area on Chicago's south side, but he had created more than 20 houses in the area around the University of Chicago, including an English Tudor house built in 1910 for Thomas Wilson, vice president of the Morris Company.

Shaw designed an English Tudor–style country house with all the associations of wealth and aristocracy that this mode of architecture can confer. In fact, Morris was a second-generation meatpacker

ENTRY GATE

EXTERIOR FROM REAR YARD

who had married a daughter of the meatpacking aristocracy. Like the exterior, the house's interiors were baronial, with wood-paneled walls and elaborately patterned plaster ceilings. Refined and handsomely detailed, the house's entry gate and projecting wings resemble those Shaw designed for the 1909–12 Finley Barrell house in Lake Forest.

Edward Morris started in his father's business at the age of 16. Morris' father, Nelson, founded his meatpacking company in 1859. During the Civil War he sold cattle to the Union Army, and by 1873, his company was grossing $11 million annually. In the early years of the last century, the Morris & Company had almost 100 branches nationwide, and in 1923 they merged with Armour & Company. At the time of his father's death in 1907, Edward was running the Morris

Company and had married Helen Swift, the daughter of Gustavus Swift, founder of Swift & Company. In addition to meatpacking, Morris held stock in many of Chicago's banks and financial institutions. He was also president of the Fairbanks Canning Company and of the St. Louis National Stock Yard Company and he was a member of the Chicago Board of Trade. His son Nelson, like Edward, took over the family business from his father. A multimillionaire playboy, Nelson married and divorced several showgirls and had the extraordinary luck to survive the crash of the *Hindenburg*. He said he heard a not very loud "bang" while sitting in the writing lounge, and when the airship collapsed in flames, he walked away from the wreck.

The house is no longer standing.

MAIN HALL AND STAIRCASE

DINING ROOM

BILLIARD ROOM

CONSERVATORY

TEA HOUSE

PERGOLA AND GARDEN

COACH HOUSE

LAKEVIEW HOUSES FOR
MRS. ARTHUR RYERSON, ABRAM POOLE,
HENRY DANGLER, AND AMBROSE CRAMER

2700–10 NORTH LAKEVIEW AVENUE

DAVID ADLER, HENRY CORWITH DANGLER, AMBROSE CRAMER, 1917

EXTERIOR OF THE FOUR TOWNHOUSES

ENTRANCE TO RYERSON HOUSE

FOUR ELEGANT ROW HOUSES, designed under the signature of "Henry Corwith Dangler, Architect," were built along Chicago's Lakeview Avenue in the Lincoln Park area between 1915 and 1917. Although the majority of Chicago's affluent families continued to live a few miles to the south on the city's Gold Coast, some prominent Chicagoans, including Mrs. Arthur Ryerson, Abram Poole, and architects Henry

Dangler and Ambrose Cramer, chose to build north, facing the park.

These four contiguous row houses bear the stamp of three architects, guided by the genius of architect David Adler. Henry Corwith Dangler was David Adler's partner when he established an office in 1911. Adler became his generation's foremost architect of Chicago country houses, but he didn't receive an architectural license until 1929

LIVING ROOM, RYERSON HOUSE

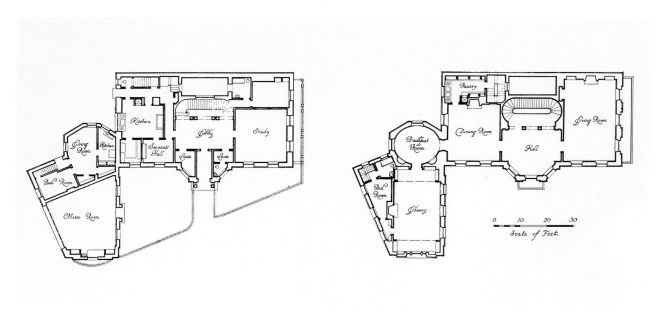

PLANS, RYERSON HOUSE

DINING ROOM, RYERSON HOUSE

and needed a partner to sign drawings. Adler chose his closest friend, Henry Dangler, who introduced Adler to his future wife, Katherine Keith (Osborne Keith's daughter), and served as best man at the Adlers' 1916 wedding.

David Adler and Henry Dangler met when they were both studying architecture at the Ecole des Beaux-Arts, introduced by Abram Poole, Adler's Princeton classmate, when Poole was also in Paris, studying painting. Before establishing their partnership, Adler and Dangler both worked in the office of the prominent country-house architect, Howard Van Doren Shaw. When Adler opened his own office, Ambrose Cramer, who was Dangler's first cousin, served as a draftsman.

Adler, Dangler, and Poole had very close personal friendships and professional relationships, resulting in this unique Adler commission. For although Dangler and Cramer clearly must have had input into their own residences, Adler scholar Stephen Salny notes that nothing left Adler's office without his final say. The architecture of these row houses reflects Adler's signature focus on symmetry, his sensitivity to scale, and his skill at exquisite detailing.

The Lakeview houses, reminiscent of Georgian squares in London and Bath, England, express Adler's talent for combining a variety of stylistic approaches. The influence of 18th-century architect Robert Adam can be found in the

MAIN HALL, POOLE HOUSE

delicately detailed fanlights over the entrance to Poole and Dangler's houses, but Adler's overall design is totally original. When this group of city houses was published in the April 1922 issue of *Architectural Forum*, the author spoke admiringly of the firm's ingenuity. He praised its ability to understand and work in a variety of styles, producing architecture "that has the spirit and charm of the definite period, yet is free from pedantic copying." Adler's work is light years away from the eclectic but somber and fussy interiors characterizing Chicago's 19th-century townhouses.

The ensemble is homogenous yet has subtle variety. All of the townhouses are faced in Flemish bond red brick, resting on a ground floor of dressed limestone, but the doorways and windows are each treated differently. Only Mrs. Ryerson's house (the largest of the four) is differentiated by pairs of exterior columns and blind arches. The interior plan of her house is further personalized by a small apartment tucked behind the irregularly shaped "motor room" (garage).

In 1912, after receiving a cablegram notifying them that their college-age son had been killed in

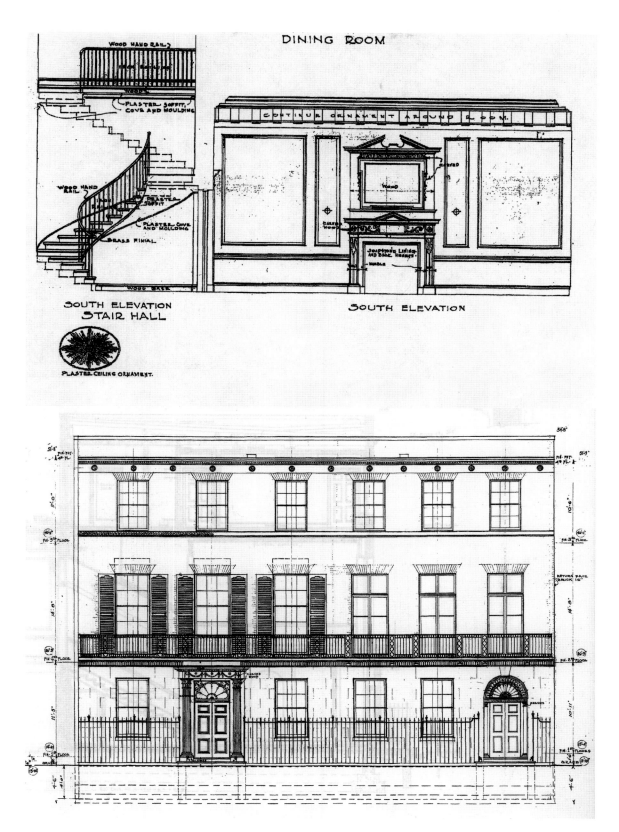

SECTION AND ELEVATION DRAWINGS, POOLE AND DANGLER HOUSES

ENTRANCE HALL, CRAMER HOUSE

DRAWING ROOM, CRAMER HOUSE

an automobile accident, the Ryersons, who had been vacationing in Europe, booked the first steamship home; it was the *Titanic,* and Arthur Larned Ryerson went down with the ship. Henry Dangler, Adler's partner, died in 1917 at age 36, ending a successful and prolific career with Adler. The owners of the other two houses were luckier. Poole enjoyed a long life as a successful painter.

After Cramer left Adler, he opened his own office, specializing in residences. He retired to Maine, where he received wide recognition for his efforts in historic preservation.

Three of the four houses have remained single-family residences. The Ryerson house has been occupied recently by a social-service agency.

FREDERICK AND ELEANOR
COUNTISS HOUSE

1524 Lake Shore Drive
Howard Van Doren Shaw, 1917

LAKE SHORE DRIVE FACADE

GROUND FLOOR, ENTRANCE LOBBY

W HEN IT WAS COMPLETED in 1917, the Countiss house was one of the last mansions to be built on the stretch of Lake Shore Drive between Oak Street and North Avenue. Once the city's northern boundary, North Avenue marked the beginning of Lincoln Park, which in 1864 had been the city cemetery. By 1917, a number of houses on Lake Shore Drive had already come down to make way for apartment buildings, including the apartment house at 1130 Lake Shore Drive, built in 1910 and designed by Howard Van Doren Shaw, whom the Countisses also selected to design their house.

Shaw was an Arts and Crafts architect who flirted with "the high game of classicism." The two Lake Forest houses Shaw designed for Edward Ryerson were classical, but Shaw's use of classical elements tended to be more original than canonical. The Arts and Crafts style of building, with its preference for simple materials, vernacular building forms, and connections to the socialist movement in England, was both too modest and too left-wing to suit Chicago's captains of industry.

Shaw's client Eleanor Robinson Countiss and her siblings spent a great deal of time in France during their childhood. Mrs. Countiss' sister

LIVING ROOM

LIBRARY

HALL AND STAIRCASE CONNECTING FIRST AND SECOND FLOORS

Laura had built her Greenwich, Connecticut, house, Northway, as a version of Ange-Jacques Gabriel's Petit Trianon at Versailles. Eleanor Countiss asked Shaw if he would also build her a version of the charming pavilion. Frank Lloyd Wright, who much later grudgingly acknowledged Shaw's talent, wrote of the Countiss house, "Another traveled rich woman adored the Petit Trianon. She must have it for a house, only it was a story too low. So Mr. Shaw put another story on the Trianon for her. If he had not done it someone else would have and would probably have done it worse. Mr. Shaw said so." Wright's derision fails to recognize Shaw's skill in the adaptation of the important features of the Petit Trianon's garden facade. Shaw transformed the Trianon's raised terrace and stone railing into the rusticated base of the Countiss house. By flattening the central giant-order columns and reproportioning the entablature and rooftop balustrade, he successfully enlarged the building vertically without destroying its proportions. For Shaw, the Petit Trianon and his adaptation were related to an urban building type he had already explored in 1911 in the William O. Goodman house.

Although the facade may be purely French-inspired, the interiors of the Countiss house combine French and English influences. Much different from the Tudor interiors of the Goodman House, the detailing here is lighter and more classical, exuding sophistication, and is comparable to David Adler's 1921 interior detailing for the Joseph Ryerson Jr. house.

The Countiss house has 30 rooms, 9 full bathrooms, 11 fireplaces, and an Otis elevator that could hold 13 people. The ground-floor entry hall is surrounded by reception rooms, a ladies' powder room, and a gentlemen's billiard room. This level has black and white checkerboard Italian marble flooring throughout. The second floor, or piano nobile, contains a living room and library that face Lake Michigan and have violet-colored marble floors and wood paneling. Here, large Oriental rugs covered the floor; they were removed for parties and dances. At the rear of this floor are the north-facing kitchen, as well as the dining room and breakfast room. The breakfast room originally held a fountain that contained goldfish, and its English cross-vaulted ceiling had the signs of the zodiac molded in plaster around a hanging birdcage. The third floor held the family bedrooms. The fourth floor contained a lake-facing guest suite for Eleanor's grandmother and servants' quarters located at the rear of the house.

Frederick Dower Countiss (1872–1926) came from a modest background. He was born in Chicago and educated in the Chicago public schools, and his father and grandfather owned grocery stores. While attending night school, he started working as a teller at the Merchant's Bank. J. Ogden Armour, who banked there, met the young Countiss and asked him to work with his nephew, S. B. Chapin, in Chapin's brokerage firm. Countiss was soon made a partner and managed the Armour and Swift accounts. In 1909–10 he served as president of the Chicago Stock Exchange.

Mrs. Countiss, Eleanor Barber Robinson, was born in Middlebury, Ohio. Her father owned the Diamond Match Company. She was one of nine children and had a twin sister who died. After her marriage, Eleanor constantly hosted parties for visiting dignitaries, organized charity events, and gave pre-opera and pre-theater dinner parties for her circle of friends. She was attractive, petite, and always dressed at the height of fashion. After she died, her children donated much of her wardrobe to the Chicago Historical Society, which featured her dresses in an exhibition of historical costumes

DINING ROOM

in 1978. During World War I, Eleanor was active in fund-raising and sold war bonds, and she served as chairperson of the Chicago chapter of the American Red Cross.

In 1923, Fred and Eleanor separated. She remained in the house she loved, and her husband moved into the Drake Hotel. Once on her own, Eleanor embarked on a professional career by starting a business producing custom-designed dresses. She then went into advertising and cosmetics, developing a liquid shampoo and a powder base that she sold to Elizabeth Arden. When she wanted a small town car, she made sketches and sent them to Henry Ford, who asked his chief designer to develop them. The Ford Motor Company made two cars from Eleanor's design; one was sent to Chicago for Mrs. Countiss' approval and the other was made for

BUTLER'S PANTRY

Ford's son Edsel. The model was later put into production.

In 1925, Eleanor Countiss' divorce was final. Using her divorce settlement, she decided to open a bank in partnership with Lawrence Harley Whiting, who had worked with her husband at Chapin & Company. The resulting Boulevard Bank was located in the Wrigley building and boasted the Wrigley Chewing Gum Company as a depositor. That same year, Eleanor married Larry Whiting and continued to live at 1524 Lake Shore Drive. Eleanor, along with Whiting, was instrumental in the conception and financing of the American Furniture Mart. Built between 1923 and 1926, it had the largest floor area of any building in the world. Whiting was given a 20-year contract to manage the Furniture Mart and held that position for the rest of his life. After Eleanor's death, when the last of the Countiss and Whiting children were out of the house, Larry Whiting moved to an apartment on Lake Shore Drive. The Eleanor Countiss Whiting house was sold in 1950 to the International College of Surgeons, who converted it into an International Museum of Surgical Science. They already owned the adjacent Edward T. Blair house, and they built a fourth-floor bridge connecting the back of the structures. Fortunately, only minimal alterations were made to the main rooms of the Countiss house. The museum is open to the public.

JOSEPH T. RYERSON JR. HOUSE

1406 Astor Street

David Adler, 1921

ASTOR STREET FACADE

GROUND FLOOR STAIR HALL

THE JOSEPH T. RYERSON JR. house, built in 1921, reflects architect David Adler's devotion to French architecture. Sophisticated and chic, the house recalls the disciplined classicism of a Louis XVI Parisian townhouse. The three-bay-wide exterior is faced with dressed limestone and appears emphatically symmetrical. The center entrance opens into a circular ground-floor reception area. Above is the grand salon, with three floor-to-ceiling pairs of French doors opening onto a shallow balcony surrounded by an ornamental wrought-iron railing. This stately home differs markedly from its more picturesque Tudor and Colonial Revival neighbors.

The simplicity of the exterior belies the house's size and its luxurious interior. Although only 40 feet wide, it contains 16,000 square feet and has 22 rooms, including seven bedrooms, nine baths, and a top-floor ballroom. Among the elegant details are a winding marble staircase with a simple wrought-iron balustrade that follows the curve of the stairs and extends through the house. Mirrors line the walls of an oval dining room. Paneling, restrained but uniquely detailed, appears in all of the major rooms. Light comes from crystal chandeliers and sconces. Through balance, consistent scale, and attention to detail, Adler achieved an elegance that eschews the more lavish and pretentious interiors

FIRST FLOOR STAIR HALL

DINING ROOM

DRAWING ROOM LOOKING SOUTH

of Chicago's high-style 19th-century houses and instead embodies the lightness and coherence found in the most beautiful salons of 18th-century Paris.

Joseph T. Ryerson Jr., born in Chicago in 1880, was a third-generation Chicagoan. His grandfather and namesake founded Joseph T. Ryerson & Son, Inc., in 1842, just nine years after Chicago was incorporated. Working his way through the company, the third Joseph Ryerson Jr. served as president from 1923 until his retirement in 1929. He continued to serve as a director when the firm became Inland Steel.

Ryerson was born into a family that valued great architecture. He married Annie Lawrie McBirney, whose parents lived in the beautiful Lake Forest estate called "House of the Four Winds" designed in 1908 by Howard Van Doren Shaw. Ryerson's father, Edward Larned Ryerson, had likewise hired Shaw, Chicago's most significant country-house architect of his generation, to design "Havenwood," the family's stunning Italian palazzo in Lake Forest. Edward Ryerson had also established a trust fund to offer fellowships to students of landscape and architecture.

David Adler was working in the office of Howard Van Doren Shaw in 1911 when he began his first commission. But it wasn't inspired by Italian or Arts and Crafts architecture; it was an imposing French château named "Pierremont" and located in Glencoe, on Chicago's North Shore.

DRAWING ROOM LOOKING TO HALL

LIBRARY

SECOND FLOOR SITTING ROOM

It was designed for his aunt and uncle, the Charles A. Stonehills.

Adler was a devoted Francophile. Like his East Coast contemporaries, Richard Morris Hunt and John Russell Pope, Adler trained at the Ecole des Beaux-Arts, where he absorbed a devotion to balance and symmetry and a keen sensitivity to proportion. He traveled widely in Europe, creating a collection of over 500 postcards, 300 of which were of French buildings. His library contained a large number of books on French architecture.

All things French were very much in vogue between the World Wars and Paris was the place to be. Children from fashionable East Coast families were frequently taught French at home and sent to the Sorbonne to finish their education. The expatriate American community in Paris in the 1920s

was lively and glittering. So it is not surprising that prominent Chicagoans such as Joseph and Annie Ryerson were drawn to French architecture for a beautiful city house in which to raise their family and entertain. Their selection of Adler was also not surprising. A *Chicago Daily News* society editor noted in a 1971 article that "as status symbols go, a David Adler House makes a Rolls Royce look like a dimestore purchase."

Joseph Ryerson's hobby was collecting "Chicagoana," and in 1931 he hired Adler to design an addition, known as the "Chicago Room," to the house. The new penthouse space accommodated Ryerson's Chicago-related books, maps, engravings, rare prints, photographs, and other materials, including his grandfather's published account describing his arrival in Chicago, his

SECOND FLOOR BEDROOM

experiences during the great Chicago fire of 1871, and the subsequent rebuilding of the city. Ryerson owned many first editions by Chicago authors, including pulp-fiction dime novels that were called "pennydreadful." His collection was donated to the Chicago Historical Society (today the Chicago Historical Museum) and the addition was removed when the house was recently restored following Adler's original design.

After Annie Ryerson's death in 1941, the Ryerson house had a series of owners, and in 1965 a legal battle ensued, leading to its subdivision into 11 apartments. In 1988, the house was sold to John Regas, who spent two years restoring it to a single-family home that now looks very much as it did when the Ryersons lived there.

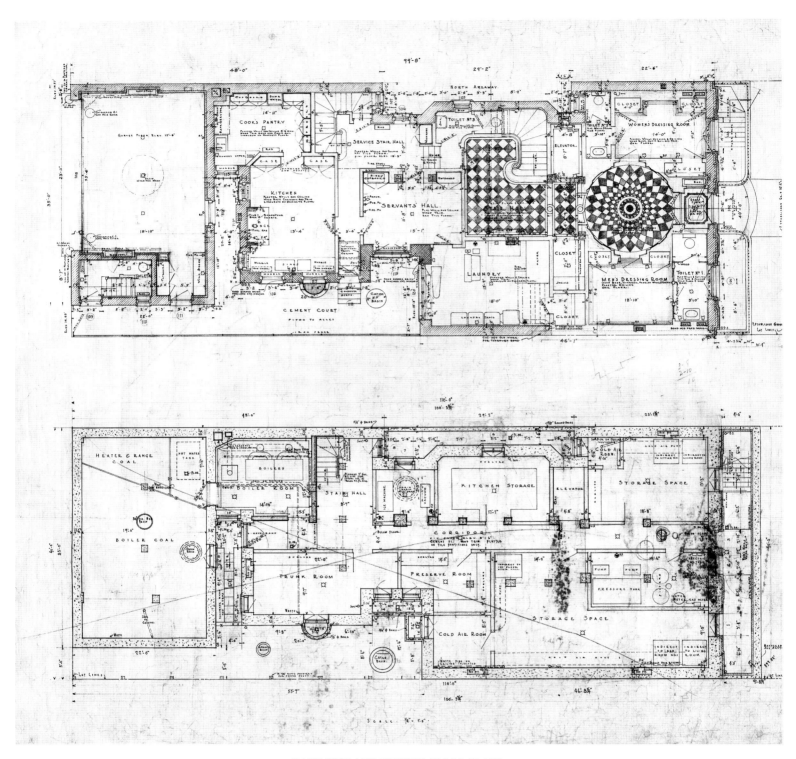

BASEMENT AND GROUND FLOOR PLANS

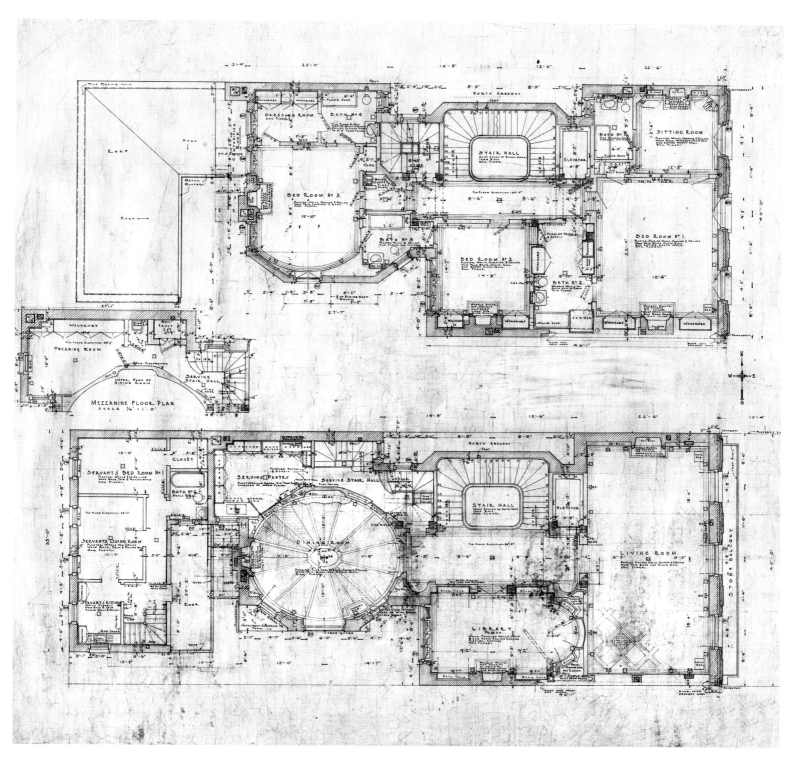

FIRST AND SECOND FLOOR PLANS

PORTFOLIO OF HOUSES

1860s. House of Robert A. Kinzie,
son of John Kinzie Chicago's first settler
Architect unknown
Demolished

1870s. House of J. Frank Aldrich, U.S. congressman,
Chicago Board of Trade
Architect unknown
Demolished

1870s. House of Philip. D. Armour, meatpacker,
Armour & Company
Architect unknown
Demolished

1874. House of Perry H. Smith, lawyer,
active in railroad management
Adolph A. Cudell, architect
Demolished

1879. House of J. J. Glessner, farm equipment manufacturer
Architect unknown; coach house designed by Isaac Scott
Demolished

1880s. House of John Mason Loomis,
lumber merchant and real estate
Francis Whitehouse, architect
Demolished

1880s. House of Emanuel Mandel of Mandel Brothers,
dry-goods merchant
Lavall B. Dixon, architect
Demolished

1880s. House of Walter C. Newberry,
Union Army General and postmaster of Chicago
William Le Baron Jenney, architect
Demolished

1881. House of Augustus Byram,
Atchinson & Nebraska Railroad Company founder
Burnham & Root, architects
Demolished

1882. Houses of Charles Farwell, U.S. Senator (left) and his brother
John V. Farwell of Farwell & Company (right),
wholesale dry goods and real estate
Treat & Foltz, architects
Demolished

1882. House of Osborne R. Keith, wholesale milliner
Lavall Dixon, architect
Demolished

1883. House of Hans Lambert Tree,
Illinois circuit judge and art collector
Peabody & Stearns, architects
Demolished

1883. House of Sidney A. Kent, meatpacker
Later owned by John "Bet a Million" Gates, stock market speculator
and founder of American Steel and Wire Company
Burnham & Root, architects
Condominiums

1884. House of Harlow Higginbotham, World's Columbian
Exposition president and partner of Marshall Field
Burling & Whitehouse, architects
Demolished

1884. House of William Borden, lawyer and mining engineer
Richard Morris Hunt, architect
Demolished

1885. House of John Cudahy, meatpacker
Francis Whitehouse, architect
Demolished

1885–86. House of Ransom R. Cable,
president of the Chicago Rock Island and Pacific Railroad Company
Cobb & Frost, architects
Offices

1886. House of Edward Partridge,
dry-goods merchant and grain trader
Wheelock & Clay, architects
Demolished

1886. House of William Hale,
president of the Hale Elevator Company and father of the
famous astronomer
Burnham & Root, architects
Condominiums

1887. House of Martin A. Ryerson, lumber baron and art collector
Treat & Foltz, architects
Religious Archive

1888. House of Conrad Seipp, brewer
Adolph Cudell, architect
Demolished

1890s. House of Victor Lawson, *Chicago Daily News* publisher
Architect unknown
Demolished

1890s. House of Alexander Caldwell McClurg, publisher
Francis Whitehouse, architect
Demolished

1890s. House of L. Hamilton McCormick,
farm equipment manufacturer
Cowles & Ohrenstein, architects
Commercial use, restaurant

1890s. House of John A. McGill, physician
Henry Ives Cobb, architect
Condominiums

1891. House of Mrs. Joseph (Louise) Bowen,
social and political activist; trustee and treasurer of Hull-House
Francis Whitehouse, architect
Demolished

1892. House of Albert Sullivan,
Illinois Central Railroad General superintendent
Adler & Sullivan, architects
Demolished

1892. House of Warren McArthur,
partner, Ham Lantern Company
Frank Lloyd Wright, architect
Private Residence

1893. House of Barbara Armour
Later owned by Harry Selfridge, partner of Marshall Field and
founder of Selfridge's in London
Francis Whitehouse, architect
Demolished

1893. House of Robert Todd Lincoln, son of President Abraham
Lincoln, lawyer, minister to Great Britain, U.S. Secretary of War, and
president of the Pullman Palace Car Company
Solon S. Beman, architect
Demolished

1896. House of Isidore Heller, meatpacker
Frank Lloyd Wright, architect
Private residence

1901. Houses of George and Frances Glessner
J. J. Glessner built this double house for his children on
Prairie Avenue
Shepley, Rutan & Coolidge, architects
Demolished

1907. House of James H. Douglas, cereal manufacturer
Howard Van Doren Shaw, architect
Private Residence

1909. House of Edwin M. Colvin, printer
George W. Maher, architect
Private residence

1910. House of R. T. Crane, plumbing fixtures manufacturer
Shepley, Rutan & Coolidge, architects
Demolished

1912. House of Edward Tyler Blair,
hardware merchant, William Blair & Company
McKim, Mead & White (William Kendall), architects
Museum, International College of Surgeons

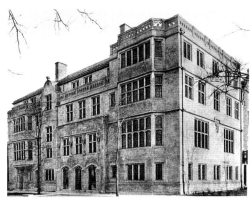

1913. House of Gustavus Swift Jr., meatpacker
Howard Van Doren Shaw, architect
Demolished

1914. House of Samuel S. Hutchinson,
Theatre Film Service Company President
Tallmadge and Watson, architects
Demolished

1914. House of Claude Seymour,
vice-president Otto Young and Company, upholsters
George Maher, architect
Private residence

1916. House of Bernard A. Eckhart,
B.A. Eckhart Milling Co. president and civic leader
Benjamin Marshall, architect
Polish Consulate

DESIGNATED LANDMARKS

APPEARING IN THIS VOLUME

PORTFOLIO

SIDNEY A. KENT HOUSE (p. 294)
National Register Landmark
Chicago Landmark

RANSOM R. CABLE HOUSE (p. 295)
Chicago Landmark

WILLIAM HALE HOUSE (p. 295)
North Kenwood Chicago Landmark District

MARTIN A. RYERSON HOUSE (p. 295)
Hyde Park-Kenwood National Register District
Kenwood Chicago Landmark District

JOHN A. MCGILL HOUSE (p. 296)
Hyde Park-Kenwood National Register District

WARREN MCARTHUR HOUSE (p. 296)
Hyde Park-Kenwood National Register District
Kenwood Chicago Landmark District

ISIDORE HELLER HOUSE (p. 297)
Hyde Park-Kenwood National Register District
Chicago Landmark

EDWIN M. COLVIN HOUSE (p. 297)
Chicago Landmark

EDWARD TYLER BLAIR HOUSE (p. 298)
Gold Coast National Register District
Seven Houses on Lake Shore Drive Chicago Landmark
District

CLAUDE SEYMOUR HOUSE (p. 298)
Buena Park National Register District
Hutchinson Street Chicago Landmark District

BERNARD A. ECKHART HOUSE (p. 298)
Gold Coast National Register District
Seven Houses on Lake Shore Drive Chicago Landmark
District

ARCHITECTS' BIOGRAPHIES

DAVID ADLER (1882–1949)

David Adler devoted his practice almost exclusively to the design of houses for elite members of Chicago society. Among his clients, Adler counted Mr. and Mrs. Joseph Ryerson Jr. (steel), Mr. and Mrs. Albert Lasker (advertising), Mr. and Mrs. William McCormick Blair (finance), and Mr. and Mrs. Lester Armour (meatpacking). Most of Adler's residences were located along Chicago's North Shore, especially in Lake Forest, but he also built houses in Chicago, for clients including Joseph T. Ryerson Jr., Mrs. Arthur Ryerson, and Charles King.

Adler was born in 1882 in Milwaukee, the son of a wealthy German-Jewish clothing manufacturer. After graduating from Princeton University in 1904, Adler studied architecture at both the Polytechnic University in Munich and the Ecole des Beaux-Arts in Paris. From Paris, he toured Europe, collecting hundreds of postcards that, along with his collection of photographs, newspaper and magazine clippings, and books, served as important sources of inspiration. Returning to Chicago in 1911, Adler went to work in the office of Howard Van Doren Shaw, a leading residential architect. A year later, Adler formed a partnership with Henry C. Dangler, a friend from the Ecole des Beaux-Arts who was also working for Shaw. After Dangler's sudden death in 1917, Adler took Robert Work, another colleague from Shaw's office, as a partner. Adler never passed the Illinois state architectural licensing exam, and both Dangler and Work, in addition to being licensed and able to sign drawings, brought their technical expertise to his projects. After Dangler's death, Adler again failed the state exam in 1917, receiving one of the lowest scores ever recorded. Asked to size the diagonal web members in a steel truss, Adler is said to have answered, "I have people in my office that attend to such matters." In 1928, with an impressive array of recommendations from clients as well as fellow architects, the examining board granted him a license. Once licensed, he never again had a partner.

Adler often collaborated with his sister Frances Elkins, who became a leading interior decorator. After his death, the *Chicago Tribune* described Adler as "a residential architect of great distinction whose taste in the decorative arts was unequalled in his time."

Architectural historian Richard Guy Wilson notes in his essay for *David Adler, Architect: The Elements of Style* that "Adler's range of stylistic choices and his quality of design and execution rank with and indeed surpass such contemporaries as John Russell Pope, Delano and Aldrich, Harrie T. Lindeberg, F. Burrell Hoffman, Jr., George Washington Smith, and Myron Hunt and Elmer Grey." He compliments their "enduring excellence."

SOLON SPENCER BEMAN (1853–1914)

Solon Spencer Beman was born in Brooklyn, New York, in 1853. His father was a roofer with an interest in architecture. In 1870, after completing elementary and secondary school, Beman went to work for the well-known New York architect Richard Upjohn. He remained in Upjohn's office until 1877, when he opened his own practice in New York City. In 1879, Beman moved from New York to Chicago, where he received the commission to design the company town of Pullman for George Pullman's expanding railroad-car manufacturing business. In the 1890s, Pullman hired him to remodel his mansion on Prairie Avenue, then Chicago's most fashionable residential street. Pullman, who had a house in Long Beach, New Jersey, met Beman through Nathan Barrett, who had landscaped Pullman's New Jersey property.

The town of Pullman was Beman's first major commission and remains his most significant work. Built over a number of years, it contained factories, an administration building, commercial and residential buildings, a hotel, a market hall, an arcade building, a steam power plant, and a water tower. It brought Beman national recognition, and he received many other commissions. In 1890, Beman built the Grand Central Station for the Chicago and Northern Pacific Railway. Over the next several years, he developed an architectural practice that consisted of luxury residences, apartment buildings, Christian Science churches, and commercial and industrial projects, including work for the Studebaker Brothers Manufacturing Company and the Pabst Brewing Company. Beman's Fine Arts Building, originally the Studebaker Building, is an early skyscraper, designed with a theater on the ground floor. Built in 1885, it remains standing on South Michigan Avenue.

EDWARD BURLING (1819–1892)
FRANCIS M. WHITEHOUSE (1848–1938)
BURLING & WHITEHOUSE

Although experienced only as a carpenter's apprentice, Edward Burling moved to Chicago in 1843 from Newburgh, New York, looking to find business as a builder. But he became, along with John Van Osdel, one of Chicago's first architects. Before Chicago's devastating 1871 fire, he had designed many residential and commercial buildings, including the First National Bank Building, the Marine Bank Building (where the Chicago Board of Trade was located), the Tribune Building, the Eli B. Williams House, Sinai Temple, Holy Name Cathedral, and St. James Episcopal Church. Following the fire, he rebuilt almost all his former commissions and supervised the construction of the customs house and the U.S. post office. Dankmar Adler, the brilliant acoustician of the Auditorium Theater and partner of Louis Sullivan, worked with Burling between 1871 and 1878. During the 1880s, Burling formed a partnership with Francis M. Whitehouse.

Francis Whitehouse was born in New York City. His father, Henry, was rector of St. Thomas Church on Fifth Avenue and was appointed the Episcopal bishop of the State of Illinois. Whitehouse studied architecture in Germany at the University of Göttingen. Returning to Chicago, where his parents had moved, he went to work for Edward Burling, who later made him his partner. In 1881, the firm of Burling & Whitehouse received the commission for the Samuel Nickerson House. They also designed the house of J. Cudahy at 23rd and Michigan Avenue. In 1882, the firm designed a new First National Bank building and in 1885 the Epiphany Episcopal Church at Adams and Ashland, a commission that came through Whitehouse's father. The firm of

Burling & Whitehouse was represented on Daniel Burnham's Board of Architects for the 1893 World's Columbian Exposition (along with such notables as McKim, Mead & White, Richard Morris Hunt, and Adler & Sullivan) and designed the fair's pier and casino. Chicago's Burling Street, which contains many houses designed by Edward Burling, bears the architect's name. Whitehouse withdrew from the firm and continued to practice as a residential architect, designing mansions on Chicago's near north side for prominent Chicagoans such as Joseph T. and Louise De Koven Bowen, Barbara Armour, and A. C. McClurg.

DANIEL HUDSON BURNHAM (1846–1912)
BURNHAM & ROOT
D. H. BURNHAM AND COMPANY

Daniel H. Burnham is best remembered as the planner of the 1893 World's Columbian Exposition in Chicago; for his city plans for Chicago, Washington, D.C., Cleveland, San Francisco, and Manila; and for his famous adage "Make no little plans; they have no magic to stir men's blood." Burnham was the first corporate architect to practice architecture on the scale of big business. According to Chicago architect Louis Sullivan, Burnham said he was "not going to stay satisfied with houses; my idea is to work up a big business, to handle big things, deal with big businessmen, and to build up a big organization."

Burnham was born in Henderson, New York and moved with his family to Chicago in 1854. He showed artistic talent early on but failed to pass the entry exams at both Harvard and Yale. Because of his son's interest in architecture, Burnham's father arranged an apprenticeship for him in the office of William Le Baron Jenney, the designer of Chicago's first metal-frame skyscraper. Burnham later worked for Carter, Drake & Wight, under

Peter B. Wight, whom Burnham regarded as a mentor.

In Wight's office Burnham met John Wellborn Root, with whom he formed a partnership that lasted until Root's premature death in 1891. Burnham & Root received their first commission from John B. Sherman, one of the founders of the Union Stock Yard and Transit Company. Burnham married Sherman's daughter. This union led to important social connections and numerous residential, small commercial, and train station commissions throughout the Midwest. In the 1880s and 1890s, the firm built iron- and steel-frame office buildings that were among the world's first skyscrapers. Burnham's most important tall buildings were the Monadnock Building, the Rookery and the Reliance buildings in Chicago, and the Flatiron Building in New York.

HENRY IVES COBB (1859–1931)
COBB & FROST

Born in Brookline, Massachusetts, Henry Ives Cobb graduated from the Lawrence Scientific School at Harvard University and then studied architecture at the Massachusetts Institute of Technology. After a year spent traveling in Europe, Cobb worked in Boston for Peabody & Stearns, whose residential work was influenced by the Shingle style made popular by H. H. Richardson and McKim, Mead & White. While working in the office of Peabody & Stearns, Cobb won a competition to design the Union Club in Chicago. In 1882 he moved to Chicago to complete the commission. Recognizing the potential for more work in the city, he contacted Charles Sumner Frost (1856–1931) to come to Chicago to join him, and the two formed a partnership. Frost was an MIT graduate who had also worked for Peabody & Stearns. Cobb & Frost were responsible for the old Chicago Opera House (demolished); the shingle and stone First Presbyterian Church, built in 1887 in the North Shore suburb of Lake Forest; and several buildings for Lake Forest University (today Lake Forest College). Cobb & Frost practiced together until 1889, when the Newberry Library wouldn't give Cobb the commission for their new building unless they had his exclusive attention. Cobb also designed the Richardsonian Romanesque old Chicago Historical Society building and the Chicago Athletic Association Building. In 1893, Cobb did the fisheries and horticulture buildings for the Chicago World's Columbian Exposition. Among Cobb's most significant Chicago commissions were buildings for the University of Chicago and mansions he designed for Potter Palmer and Dr. John A. McGill. Cobb was elected a fellow of the American Institute of Architects in 1889. In 1898, Cobb moved to New York, where he practiced until his death in 1931.

ADOLPH CUDELL (1850–1910)
ARTHUR HERCZ (1866–1941)
CUDELL & BLUMENTHAL

Adolph Cudell was born in Aix-la-Chapelle and educated in Germany. He came to Chicago shortly after the great Chicago fire of 1871 and formed the firm of Cudell & Blumenthal. Richard E. Schmidt, known for having designed the Albert Madlener house and the Montgomery Ward Warehouse, which he began when working for Cudell. Schmidt remembered Cudell as a talented draftsman influenced by the Neo-Grec style of the 19th century. Cudell designed a number of residences for prominent Chicagoans, including Perry H. Smith, Cyrus McCormick, and Conrad Seipp.

Cudell later worked with Arthur Hercz, who was born in 1866 in Hungary, studied in Vienna,

and won a three-year scholarship to study in Rome. In 1892 he came to Chicago to work on the World's Columbian Exposition, serving as a draftsman in the office of Burnham & Root. He designed several structures for the German exhibition at the fair. In 1894 he formed a partnership with Cudell to design the Francis Dewes Mansion. Four years later, he and sculptor Max Mach won a U.S. competition to design a monument to Lafayette in France. In his later career, Cudell became a designer and manufacturer of cabinetry and fine furniture.

EMIL H. FROMMANN (c. 1862–1950)
FROMMANN & JEBSEN

Emil Frommann was born in Illinois circa 1862 but came from a German background, as did his wife. Although he lived modestly compared to some of his wealthy clients, he seems to have had an active practice under the firm name Frommann & Jebsen. The firm designed small apartment buildings and single-family houses, as well as a stable building in Chicago's Humboldt Park. Completed in 1896, it resembled an old German country house. His best-known work was done for members of Chicago's large German community, and his clients included Hermann Paepke and Edward Uihlein. In 1903, Frommann & Jebsen designed a rambling Queen Anne estate house in Glencoe for lumber magnate Paepke. Uihlein was a particularly loyal client, hiring the firm to design his own house in Wicker Park and, before Prohibition in the 1920s, many saloons throughout Chicago for the Schlitz Brewing Company.

CHARLES SUMNER FROST (1856–1931)
COBB and FROST
FROST and GRANGER

Charles Sumner Frost was born in Lewiston, Maine, and worked for his father, who was a builder, lumber merchant, and owner of a lumber mill. He apprenticed for an architect in Lewiston briefly before attending the Massachusetts Institute of Technology, from which he graduated in 1876. He worked in Boston for Peabody & Stearns until 1881 and then moved to Chicago, entering into practice with Henry Ives Cobb, with whom he had worked at Peabody & Stearns. The buildings Frost designed in the 1890s included a substantial residence for George A. Fuller, head of a major Chicago construction company; several other Chicago houses; and the Kenwood and Calumet clubs. In 1898, after practicing alone for nine years, Frost formed a partnership with his brother-in-law, Alfred Granger. It is thought that Granger was the design partner. Both men married daughters of Marvin Hewitt, the president of the Chicago and North Western Railway. Known primarily for their design of railroad stations, Frost & Granger had commissions including the Chicago and North Western terminal, as well as stations in St. Paul, Minnesota, and Omaha, Nebraska. Frost & Granger also built an office building for the Chicago and North Western Railway. They designed many buildings at Lake Forest University (later Lake Forest College). In 1916 Frost designed Chicago's Navy Pier. Originally a member of the Western Association of Architects, which merged with the American Institute of Architects, Frost was elected a fellow of the AIA.

ALFRED HOYT GRANGER (1867–1939)
FROST and GRANGER

Alfred H. Granger was born in Zanesville, Ohio and attended Kenyon College. He studied architecture at the Massachusetts Institute of Technology, graduating in 1887, and then at the Ecole des Beaux-Arts. After he returned from Paris, Granger joined the Boston office of Shepley, Rutan & Coolidge, the successors to H. H. Richardson's firm. While working on the firm's commissions for the Chicago Public Library and the Art Institute of Chicago in the early 1890s, Granger was sent to Chicago to supervise construction. He remained in Chicago and formed a partnership with Frank B. Meade for four years before setting up a firm with Charles S. Frost. Granger's partnership with Frost ended in 1910, when he moved to Philadelphia. Returning to Chicago in 1924, Granger established the firm of Granger, Lowe, & Bollenbacher, which later became Granger & Bollenbacher. The firm designed the medical and dental building for the University of Illinois at Chicago, Pierce Hall at Kenyon College, and the administration and student union building at the University of Indiana. In 1922, Granger chaired the jury for the international competition for a new headquarters building for the *Chicago Tribune*. Like his former partner, Charles Frost, Granger was active in the American Institute of Architects, serving as president of the Chicago chapter. He was elected a fellow of the AIA in 1926. Granger authored two important books, a 1913 biography of Charles McKim and, in 1933, a notable guide to the city's architecture, *Chicago Welcomes You*.

ARTHUR HEUN (1866–1946)

Born in Saginaw, Michigan, Arthur Heun began his career in architecture as an apprentice to his uncle, Volusin Bude, who practiced architecture in Grand Rapids. Heun moved to Chicago at the age of 21 and went to work for Francis Whitehouse, a residential architect who counted among his clients such prominent Chicagoans as book publisher A. C. McClurg. When Whitehouse retired in 1893, Heun took over his office.

Heun enjoyed a major practice in the design of North Shore country houses. In 1908, he designed Mellody Farm in Lake Forest (1904–8) for J. Ogden Armour, as well as places for Charles Pike and Arthur Meeker Sr. Heun had an office in Dwight Perkins' Steinway Hall (1905) on the floor below the studio shared by Walter Burley Griffin; Spencer & Powers; Frank Lloyd Wright's former partner, Webster Tomlinson; William Drummond, Wright's chief draftsman; and Pond & Pond. Heun was included in "the Eighteen," a dining club of Chicago's young turks who met monthly to discuss architecture. In addition to residences, Heun designed the Casino Club in Chicago.

RICHARD MORRIS HUNT (1827–1895)

Richard Morris Hunt was known in his time as the dean of American architecture. He was the first American to attend the Ecole des Beaux-Arts in Paris and promoted the studio teaching method of the Ecole in American education. He was a founder of the American Institute of Architects and served as its secretary and then president.

Hunt was born in Brattleboro, Vermont. His father was a wealthy lawyer who served as a congressman. Hunt attended a Quaker school in Sandwich, Massachusetts and then the Boston Latin School. The year after his father died (1883), his mother took the family to live in Europe. Hunt attended school in Geneva, Switzerland and studied architectural drawing. Originally he considered going into the military but decided on architecture instead. Hunt attended the Ecole des Beaux-Arts beginning in 1845, finally completing his studies in 1854. In Paris he worked for his teacher Hector Lefuel as an inspector of works for Lefuel's alterations to the Louvre. In 1855 Hunt returned to New York to open his office. Along with his professional practice, Hunt ran a studio that offered instruction in architectural design. Among his students were Charles Gambrill, George B. Post, Henry Van Brunt, and Frank Furness.

Hunt's prominent New York City commissions included the Lenox Library, additions to and remodeling of the original structure of the Metropolitan Museum, and the design of the pedestal for the Statue of Liberty. He also designed the Fogg Museum at Harvard University in Cambridge. Hunt was well known for his residential works, which were predominantly designed in the style of French Renaissance châteaux. Among his New York commissions were mansions for John Jacob Astor and William K. Vanderbilt. In Newport, Rhode Island, he built The Breakers for Cornelius Vanderbilt and Marble House for William K. Vanderbilt. His largest and most famous house was Biltmore (1888–95), a 235-room residence built for George W. Vanderbilt on 125,000 acres at Asheville, North Carolina. In Chicago, Hunt designed houses for Marshall Field and William Borden. He also served as chairman of the Board of Architects for the 1893 Chicago World's Columbian Exposition and designed the fair's Administration Building.

GEORGE WASHINGTON MAHER
(1846–1926)

George W. Maher was born in Mill Creek, West Virginia. His family moved to New Albany, Indiana, and then to Chicago, but Maher's father could not find work. The young Maher had to support himself, and in 1883 he joined the architectural firm of Bauer & Hill. He then worked for Joseph Lyman Silsbee, a fashionable residential architect who employed Frank Lloyd Wright and George Grant Elmslie as draftsmen at the same time that Maher worked in the office. In 1889, Maher opened his own practice and was briefly in partnership with Charles Corwin. In 1892, Maher met J. L. Cochran, who was developing Edgewater, which had been incorporated into the City of Chicago in 1889. Cochran hired Maher to design houses for Edgewater, a move that launched Maher's successful career as a residential architect. In 1893 he built a house for himself in the North Shore suburb of Kenilworth, where he later designed a number of houses as well as the Kenilworth Club. One of his most eloquent designs was for Pleasant Home, built in Oak Park, Illinois, in 1897 for John Farson. It is a National Historic Landmark open to the public. In addition to his suburban residential commissions, Maher continued to design houses in Chicago, including those for John Rath and E. J. Magerstadt. Hutchinson Street in Chicago, originally called Kenesaw Terrace, has several large houses designed by Maher. His clients on the street included John C. Scales, Claude Seymour, Edwin J. Mosser, Grace Brackebush, and William H. Lake. Maher also designed several commercial and institutional buildings. At Northwestern University he designed the Patten Gymnasium and the Swift Hall of Engineering. The last of Maher's large major commercial commissions was the Winona

Savings Bank (1915), a result of his reputation for the work he had done for the J. R. Watkins Medical Company of Winona, Minnesota.

Maher was active in the American Institute of Architects and elected a fellow in 1916. During the early 1920s he acted as chairman of the committee for the restoration/reconstruction of the Palace of Fine Arts, designed by Charles Atwood of D. H. Burnham and Company for the 1893 World's Columbian Exposition. The actual work was not begun, however, until 1929, after Maher's death. It was completed in 1934, and the building now houses Chicago's Museum of Science and Industry.

CHARLES FOLLEN MCKIM (1847–1909)
WILLIAM RUTHERFORD MEAD
(1846–1928)
STANFORD WHITE (1853–1906)
MCKIM, MEAD & WHITE

McKim, Mead & White was the country's largest, most prominent, and most influential architectural firm practicing at the beginning of the 20th century. The firm's portfolio, including early projects and later work produced by their junior partners, numbered nearly 1,000 completed commissions. The practice was instrumental in the success of the Classical Revival style that flourished following the 1893 Chicago World's Fair. All three partners collaborated on the design of the firm's buildings. Each managed his individual projects and Mead was responsible for the management of the office.

Charles McKim was born in Chester County, Pennsylvania. His father was an important abolitionist. McKim attended public school and then studied for a year at the Lawrence Scientific School at Harvard University, originally planning on becoming a mining engineer. After he decided to become an architect, he went to New York to apprentice in the office of Russell Sturgis. He continued his education, spending three years at the Ecole des Beaux-Arts in Paris and traveling throughout Europe. After returning to the United States in 1870, he took a position in the office of Gambrill & Richardson, working with H. H. Richardson on the design for the Brattle Square Church in Boston. McKim soon set up his own office, designing houses for friends, and in 1872, when William Mead returned from touring Europe, he asked Mead to join his practice. In 1878 the two men were joined by William Bigelow, who practiced with them for only a year. Bigelow was replaced the following year by Stanford White. McKim was made a fellow of the American Institute of Architects (AIA) and received the gold medal of the Royal Institute of British Architects. He was awarded the AIA gold medal posthumously. McKim was instrumental in founding the American Academy in Rome and served as its first president.

William Mead was born in Brattleboro, Vermont, and studied at Amherst College, graduating in 1867. After graduation, he went to New York and, like McKim, apprenticed in the office of Russell Sturgis. After leaving Sturgis' office, he spent a year and a half traveling in Europe. He returned to New York in 1872 and joined Charles McKim in practice. Mead was made a fellow of the American Institute of Architects and was elected to the Academy of Arts and Letters, and in 1909, after McKim's death, succeeded him as president of the American Academy in Rome.

Stanford White was born in New York City. His father, Richard Grant White, was a noted critic of art, music, and literature and a Shakespearean scholar. White attended private school and graduated from New York University. An accomplished artist, the young White was per-

suaded not to pursue art as a profession, and in 1872 his father's friend Frederick Law Olmsted arranged a position for him with H. H. Richardson. White was 19 when he went to work for Gambrill & Richardson in New York. He soon became Richardson's chief assistant, executing many of the published renderings of Richardson's buildings, including one of the Watts Sherman House in Newport, Rhode Island. In 1878, White left to travel in Europe, meeting McKim in France, where the two traveled together. When White returned to New York in 1880, he was asked to join McKim and Mead in practice.

The Boston Public Library, McKim, Mead & White's first large significant public commission, was won in a competition held in 1887. Other influential buildings designed by the firm included the Casino in Newport, Rhode Island, and Madison Square Garden and Pennsylvania Station (demolished) in New York City. The firm completed the plan and principal buildings for Columbia University in New York and buildings at the University of Virginia, West Point, Radcliffe College, and Harvard University. McKim, Mead & White also worked on alterations and additions to the White House in Washington, D.C.

Although best known for their civic and institutional commissions, McKim, Mead & White had a very successful residential practice. They initially produced Shingle style houses in the manner of H. H. Richardson, for whom both McKim and White had worked, but their later houses were in the Italian Renaissance style that the firm was to champion. Their highly original Shingle style house (demolished) for William G. Lowe (1886), in Bristol, Rhode Island, has been made, through the writings of architectural historian Vincent Scully and architect Robert Venturi, into an icon of American architecture. The firm's influential residential clients included Henry Villard, Joseph Pulitzer, William C. Whitney, John Jacob Astor, Charles Dana Gibson, Charles Tiffany, George Eastman, and, in Chicago, Robert W. Patterson, Bryan Lathrop, and Edward T. Blair. The firm also built a vacation house in Richfield Springs, New York in 1883 for Cyrus McCormick Sr. of Chicago.

GEORGE C. NIMMONS (1865–1947)
WILLIAM K. FELLOWS (1870–1948)
NIMMONS & FELLOWS

George Nimmons was born in Wooster, Ohio, where he received his initial schooling, and he later studied in Europe. After returning to the United States, he went to work in Chicago for Burnham & Root at the age of 18. He remained with that firm as a draftsman for 10 years.

William Fellows was born and educated in Winona, Minnesota. He studied architecture at Columbia University and worked in various New York architectural offices. Fellows then won a European traveling fellowship. When he returned from abroad he moved to Chicago, where he formed a partnership with George Nimmons in 1897. One of their most important commissions was the huge complex the firm designed in 1906 for Sears, Roebuck & Company, which became the world's largest mail-order business under the leadership of Julius Rosenwald. Its nine-story merchandise building had a floor area of 1.7 million square feet. (The property has been redeveloped, and today only the building's tower remains). Nimmons & Fellows became the company's architects, designing buildings for Sears, Roebuck across the Midwest. In 1903, they designed Rosenwald's Hyde Park house, one of their few residential commissions. Nimmons & Fellows were considered Prairie School architects, even though they were best known for their

industrial work. They practiced together until 1910, when Fellows partnered with Dwight Perkins and John Hamilton, forming Perkins, Fellows, & Hamilton. This firm specialized in the design of schools. Between 1910 and 1917, Nimmons practiced alone. In 1914 he designed a stunning warehouse building for Reid, Murdoch & Co. Nimmons later formed the firm of Nimmons, Carr & Wright.

IRVING K. POND (1857–1939)
ALLEN B. POND (1858–1929)
POND & POND

Although Irving and Allen Pond designed many fashionable residences, they were best known for their association with Jane Addams' Hull-House in Chicago and their interest in social reform. They designed 10 buildings over an 18-year period as additions to the original Hull-House, which was built as a home for General Charles J. Hull, in 1856. Allen Pond served as secretary of Hull-House from 1895 until his death. Born in Ann Arbor, Michigan, both brothers attended the University of Michigan. Upon graduating, Allen taught at Ann Arbor High School and Michigan State University. He also worked as an assistant to his father, who was warden at the Michigan State Prison in Jackson. Irving graduated from the University of Michigan with a degree in civil engineering. It was at Michigan that he met William Le Baron Jenney who traveled up from Chicago to teach there. Pond subsequently worked in Chicago for Jenney. Irving then joined the office of Solon Spencer Beman, working on the design for the town of Pullman. The brothers formed a partnership in 1886 and practiced together until Allen's death in 1929. In Chicago they built the Baptist Training School for Nurses, the City Club, and Presbyterian churches in Chicago's community areas of Ravenswood and Hyde Park. They also designed buildings for several midwestern universities, including the student union buildings at the University of Michigan and Purdue University, as well as campus buildings for Lake Forest University (1892–94), later Lake Forest College. Both brothers were fellows of the American Institute of Architects. Irving was active in the AIA and was elected its national president in 1908, succeeding New York architect Cass Gilbert. He also wrote extensively about architecture for various journals and, in 1918, published *Meaning in Architecture,* a book on architectural theory.

HENRY HOBSON RICHARDSON
(1838–1886)

H. H. Richardson was one of America's greatest 19th-century architects, considered by many to be the most creative and prominent practitioner of his generation. His buildings were initially designed in the Romanesque Revival style, and the numerous structures they influenced in America and abroad came to be known as Richardsonian Romanesque. In Chicago, his work had an impact on the architecture of Henry Ives Cobb, John Wellborn Root and Louis Sullivan. By the 1890s, "Richardsonian" was a national style.

Richardson was born near New Orleans, Louisiana. His father was a cotton merchant. His mother was a great-granddaughter of the scientist Joseph Priestly, who discovered oxygen. Richardson attended private schools in New Orleans and was sent to Harvard University. Talented at both mathematics and drawing, Richardson decided to become an architect. After graduation from Harvard in 1860, he attended the Ecole des Beaux-Arts in Paris. He was only

the second American, after Richard Morris Hunt, to do so. With the outbreak of the Civil War at home, Richardson was forced to support himself in Paris and worked in the architecture studio of Henri Labrouste's brother Jacques. He returned to the United States in 1865, just after the war, but decided not to go back to the South; rather, he settled in New York. In 1867 he married and moved to Staten Island, New York, where he established a partnership with Charles Gambrill. Many of Richardson's early commissions, which established his reputation, were won in competitions. In 1870 he was awarded the commission for the Brattle Square Church in Boston. This was the first of his buildings done in the Romanesque style. Richardson was attracted to the Romanesque architecture of central France. He saw in it an elemental masonry architecture of walls and arches, an architecture of simplicity and great visual strength.

In 1872, Richardson won the competition for Boston's Trinity Church, a commission that brought him national prominence. In 1874, after terminating his partnership with Gambrill, he moved to a house in Brookline, Massachusetts. The following year Richardson was asked to work on the New York State Capitol building at Albany, a commission that paired him with the landscape architect Frederick Law Olmsted. They became lifelong friends, Olmsted having an influence on Richardson's perception of the American landscape and its relationship to architecture. This perception influenced many of his later designs for stone buildings, which have an almost geological presence. The core of Richardson's practice was churches, city halls, and public libraries, with the Allegheny County Courthouse and Jail (1883–88) in Pittsburgh as his masterpiece. Of almost equal influence was the Marshall Field Wholesale Store, designed in Chicago in 1885. This building (demolished) was admired by Louis Sullivan for its function, simplicity, and eloquence. Although Richardson was not thought of as a residential architect, nearly 40 percent of his practice consisted of highly original houses built for prominent and powerful clients. Among them were city houses in Washington, D.C., for John Hay, Secretary of State under William McKinley; Henry Adams; and John J. Glessner's business partner, Benjamin Warder. Richardson designed houses in Chicago for Glessner and Franklin MacVeagh (1886), as well as numerous suburban houses in the Boston area. The John J. Glessner House is the only remaining building designed by Richardson in Chicago and one of his greatest houses.

Richardson's impact on the profession and on American architecture was profound, and many notable architects, including Charles Follen McKim, Stanford White, and Chicago architect Dwight Perkins, trained in his office.

JAMES GAMBLE ROGERS (1867–1947)

James G. Rogers was born in 1867 at Bryant's Station, Kentucky, but grew up on the north side of Chicago. He earned a scholarship to Yale University and, after graduation, traveled through Europe as part of an American exhibition baseball team that introduced the sport to the Continent. Once back in Chicago in 1889, he worked for William Le Baron Jenney, and then for Burnham & Root. This was his only architectural training before opening his own firm. He practiced briefly and then went to Paris in 1892 to study at the Ecole des Beaux-Arts. Upon returning to Chicago, he reopened his architectural practice. Early commissions included modest-sized, half-timbered Tudor style resi-

dences. Rogers married Anne Day, the daughter of Albert Morgan Day, president of the Chicago Stock Exchange. Albert Day was related to the McCormick family through his wife and Anne's sister married Francis C. Farwell, a member of one of Chicago's oldest families. John V. Farwell had been Marshall Field's partner in the dry-goods business and owned vast amounts of property in Chicago. Farwell later headed the committee for Yale University's campus plan. These family connections led to Rogers' Chicago and Lake Forest residential commissions, including the Dr. George Isham house, and some of his later academic buildings.

In 1905, Rogers moved his office from Chicago to New York, attracted by the prospect of larger commissions that could be secured through East Coast friends from his college days at Yale.

The building that launched his New York career was the lavish mansion he designed for Edward Harkness, whose family fortune came from early investments in, and 15 percent ownership of, John D. Rockefeller's Standard Oil Company. Rogers' relationship with the Harkness family led to important public and institutional commissions throughout his career. He is best known for the university buildings he designed, particularly at Yale, where he was responsible for the Harkness Memorial Quadrangle, Harkness Tower, and the Sterling Memorial Library, a commission he received after the original architect, Bertram Goodhue, died. Rogers also designed Yale's Sterling Law buildings, the Hall of Graduate Studies, and eight residential colleges. At Northwestern University in Evanston, Illinois, he designed the Deering Library and the Sorority Quadrangle. Rogers also designed buildings at the University of Chicago, Princeton, and Columbia. Rogers played a particularly significant role in the

American development of what became known as the Collegiate Gothic style.

JOHN WELLBORN ROOT (1850–1891)
BURNHAM & ROOT

John Wellborn Root was arguably the most important Chicago architect of his generation. Six years older than Louis Sullivan, Root was born in Lumpkin, Georgia. He was sent to school in Liverpool, England, during the Civil War, returning to America in 1866. He graduated from New York University in 1869 with a degree in civil engineering. After working in New York for James Renwick, he moved to Chicago in 1872 to take a position with Peter B. Wight, whose office had a lively practice rebuilding the city after the 1871 Chicago fire. Daniel Burnham also went to work in Wight's firm, Carter, Drake & Wight.

In 1873, Burnham & Root both left Wight to open their own office. Burnham organized and managed their successful practice, and Root functioned as the firm's chief designer. Burnham & Root remained in practice for 18 years, before Root's death at the age of 41.

John Wellborn Root's first skyscraper, the 10-story Montauk Block (1881), was one of the earliest buildings to be supported by an iron structural frame of columns and beams, although its exterior wall was constructed of load-bearing masonry. This building also pioneered the use of grillage footings, and steel rails encased in concrete. Wight, who claims to have invented this type of footing, acted as a consultant to his two former employees. Root's artistic masterpieces are the Rookery (1888) and the Monadnock Building (1891). Both remain standing and are two of the city's most significant Chicago School buildings. The character of the Rookery's extraordinary iron and glass atrium did not survive Frank Lloyd

Wright's 1905 remodeling of the space. Boston developer Peter Brooks, who commissioned the Monadnock Building, didn't believe that the "new" technique of constructing tall buildings with steel frames would endure. He urged Root to design an office building devoid of costly ornament. Root's design, the tallest masonry-bearing-wall building in the world, is an elegant, tapering monolith with undulating bay windows. The prolific firm of Burnham & Root designed office buildings, hotels, apartment buildings, train stations, churches, schools, hospitals, and over 200 private residences.

Root was an active and influential member of Chicago's cultural community. He wrote articles on architectural theory for *Inland Architect* and theater and music reviews for Chicago newspapers. In 1884 he was an organizer of the Western Association of Architects, which later merged with the American Institute of Architects. Root was elected national secretary of the AIA and served in this capacity until his death.

RICHARD E. SCHMIDT (1856–1951)
HUGH M. G. GARDEN (1873–1961)
EDGAR MARTIN (1875–1951)
SCHMIDT, GARDEN & MARTIN

Richard E. Schmidt was born in Ebern, Germany and came to America with his family as an infant. He attended Chicago public schools and then enrolled at the Massachusetts Institute of Technology, where he studied architecture from 1883 to 1885. He began his architectural practice in 1887. Many of Schmidt's early buildings were done in collaboration with Hugh Garden, who worked for him as a freelance designer.

Hugh M. G. Garden, the son of a civil engineer, was born in Toronto, Canada, in 1873. He attended the Bishop College School in Lennoxville, Quebec, but left school at the age of 14 after his father died. His family moved to Minneapolis, and Garden, who had a talent for drawing, found work as an apprentice to William Channing Whitney, a local architect. Garden then moved to Chicago, where he worked for Flanders & Zimmerman, Henry Ives Cobb, and the Chicago office of Shepley, Rutan & Coolidge. During the economic depression following the 1893 World's Fair, Garden did freelance design work and made architectural renderings for a number of architects, including Alfred Granger, Howard Van Doren Shaw, Richard E. Schmidt, Louis Sullivan, and Frank Lloyd Wright. Garden's name, along with that of Wright's early collaborator Charles Corwin, appears on the rendering of Wright's Cheltenham Beach project that was published in 1895. A talented designer, Garden worked on a number of projects for Richard Schmidt, who, in 1895, invited Garden to be his partner. Although Garden agreed he continued to maintain his own office space until 1899. Garden had a steady, distinguished practice for three decades, alone and with his partners, designing country houses in Lake Forest and other North Shore suburbs. He frequently worked with landscape architect Jens Jensen. Schmidt and Garden were joined by Edgar Martin, an architect and structural engineer, who later formed a partnership with Pond & Pond. In *The Prairie School,* H. Allen Brooks described Garden's work as "some of the finest designs of the period . . . sharing Sullivan's concern for a strong positive massing, simplification of basic forms, and careful attention to the relation between solid and void." Among Schmidt, Garden & Martin's best-known works are the Schoenhofen Brewery, Michael Reese Hospital, and the Montgomery Ward & Company Warehouse Building, which is considered one of the canonical buildings of the Chicago School of architecture. While employed by Schmidt, Hugh Garden designed the Albert F. Madlener house, now the Graham Foundation headquarters.

HOWARD VAN DOREN SHAW
(1869–1926)

Howard Van Doren Shaw was the leading residential architect of his generation in the Chicago area. In 1926, he was awarded the Gold Medal of the American Institute of Architects. At the time, he was one of only nine American architects to have been granted the highest award bestowed by the AIA and the only residential architect so unanimously respected by his peers. Shaw was born in Chicago in 1869. He attended Yale University, graduating in 1890, and then studied architecture at the Massachusetts Institute of Technology. After graduating in 1892, he worked in Chicago for Jenney & Mundie, the firm established by William LeBaron Jenney, where many Chicago School architects, including Louis Sullivan, had trained. In 1893 he married Frances Wells, his childhood sweetheart, and opened his own architectural practice.

Shaw's first independent commission was a house built in Connecticut for Frances' father. Shaw set up an office on the top floor of his father's house in Hyde Park near the University of Chicago. He employed as his first draftsman Robert Work, who would later be a partner in David Adler's practice. Shaw began by designing adjoining townhouses in Hyde Park for his family and for Frances' sister and her husband. He built a number of residences in Hyde Park, including houses for Shaw's family friends. Yale ties and club memberships brought him residential commissions from many of Chicago's most prominent families, including the Ryersons (steel) and the Donnelleys (printing). For Reuben Donnelley, the father of a friend from Yale, he built the Lakeside Press building in Chicago. In

1916, Shaw designed Market Square in Lake Forest, considered one of the country's earliest shopping centers. He also designed Marktown, Indiana, a model town for steelworkers, similar in concept to Pullman, for Shaw's residential client Clayton Mark, who owned Mark Steel. He designed Lake Shore Country Club in Glencoe, Illinois, the Quadrangle Club at the University of Chicago, and commissions for the Art Institute of Chicago, where he was a trustee. He designed the Burnham Library and the Goodman Theater (demolished) for the museum. On State Street, he designed the Mentor Building where his office was located. Shaw renovated James Renwick's Second Presbyterian Church on South Michigan Avenue in Chicago, and, in 1914, worked with Ralph Adams Cram designing the cloister of the Fourth Presbyterian Church on North Michigan Avenue. He designed the apartment building at 1130 Lake Shore Drive, where he lived on the top floor until 1923, when he moved into an apartment at 2450 Lakeview Avenue, another of his designs.

Shaw's early work in Chicago was done in the English Tudor style. Most of Shaw's later houses were free compositions of traditional residential elements reminiscent largely of English and occasionally of Italian architecture. The English Arts and Crafts movement had an important influence on him, as it did on the Prairie School architects, and Arts and Crafts detailing may be found in many Shaw interiors.

GEORGE F. SHEPLEY (1860–1903)
CHARLES H. RUTAN (1851–1919)
CHARLES A. COOLIDGE (1858–1936)
SHEPLEY, RUTAN & COOLIDGE

Upon H. H. Richardson's death in 1886, George Shepley, Charles Rutan, and Charles Coolidge inherited his architectural practice and unfinished work. All three had been longtime employees of Richardson's. Rutan began his apprenticeship with Gambrill & Richardson when he was only 18 years old. Shepley attended Washington University and then studied architecture at MIT before joining Richardson's office in 1882. Coolidge attended Harvard and MIT, joining Richardson's office in 1883. Shepley, Rutan & Coolidge's earliest buildings, the New Orleans Public Library (1887) and the Lionberger Warehouse (1887) in St. Louis, were in the Romanesque style associated with H. H. Richardson. They went on to establish a national reputation in their own right, and their later designs were neoclassical, reflecting the influence of McKim, Mead, & White. They designed the Stanford University campus in Palo Alto (1892) and the Ames Building (1892), then the tallest building in Boston and the second-tallest bearing-wall building in America. Among their other works were the Chicago Public Library (1894), Perkins Hall at Harvard (1897), the Art Institute of Chicago (1897), the Chapel at Vassar College (1903), and the John Hay Library at Brown University (1907). In 1886, George Shepley married Richardson's daughter Julia. Following the deaths of Shepley and Rutan, Charles Coolidge reorganized the firm as Coolidge, Shepley, Bulfinch & Abbott, making Shepley's son Henry Richardson Shepley a partner. The firm, now called Shepley, Bulfinch, Richardson & Abbott, is still in practice today.

LOUIS SULLIVAN (1856–1924)

Louis Sullivan is remembered today as one of Chicago's most significant early architects. He was an important Chicago figure in the search for an American architecture and is considered by historians as one of the pioneers of 20th-century modern architecture. He is known as much for his theoretical writings as for his buildings. An admirer of H. H. Richardson, Sullivan built civic buildings in the Romanesque style. The development of his personal artistic style is reflected in his design for the Transportation Building at the 1893 World's Fair, although it was still based on the simplified arched motifs of Romanesque architecture. In his quest for a new, "modern" architecture that didn't rely on historical styles, Sullivan must have realized the necessity of abandoning the canonized rules governing the choice, arrangement, and proportion of architectural elements. The result of these rules was to give each building a visual unity in which all the parts were related to the entire building. Sullivan turned to decorative ornamental motifs repeated throughout his buildings at different locations and scales to provide this visual unity. Nicholas Pevsner, an important historian of early 20th-century architecture, saw Sullivan's ornament as related to the development of Art Nouveau. However, it was clearly derived from the leaf and berry motifs of Romanesque ornament. Frank Lloyd Wright became a champion of Sullivan's work and his reputation and wrote *Genius and the Mobocracy*, a biography of Sullivan. Wright saw in Sullivan's ideas about ornament the possibility of unifying, through repetition, all the parts of a building—its plan, volume, massing, openings, and ornament. Sullivan also played an important role in the development of the skyscraper in Chicago. In an article titled "The Tall Office Building Artistically Considered," first published in *Lippincott's Magazine* (March 1896), Sullivan described the column, with its base, shaft, and capital, as an artistic model for the design of tall buildings. The article also contained his famous dictum "Form follows function." However, it was not the objec-

tive engineering aspects of architecture, but the artistic and spiritual, on which Sullivan placed the greatest value.

Louis Sullivan was born in 1856 in Boston, Massachusetts where he attended public school. His father, Patrick, who immigrated to Boston from Ireland in 1847, opened a music and dance academy. Sullivan's mother, Anna List, was a landscape painter and musician. Sullivan, who claimed he knew he wanted to be an architect at the age of 13, studied architecture at MIT. Dissatisfied with the course of study, he left and went to work for Frank Furness in Philadelphia, where his family had relatives. He remained in the office of Furness & Hewitt for about a year. Sullivan's parents and brother Albert had moved to Chicago, and Sullivan joined them. He went to work in the office of William Le Baron Jenney.

On the advice of the architect Richard Morris Hunt, America's foremost proponent of French architectural education, Sullivan left Chicago in 1874 to study in Paris at the Ecole des Beaux-Arts. After two years, he returned to Chicago and took a job with Dankmar Adler. In 1881, Sullivan became Adler's chief draftsman and in 1883 was made a partner in the firm of Adler & Sullivan as the firm's designer. Their tour-de-force buildings were the Auditorium Building (1886–89) and the Chicago Stock Exchange Building (1883, demolished). In 1895, during a national depression, Adler withdrew from the partnership. Among Sullivan's most significant designs are the facade of the Gage Building (1899), one of three adjacent buildings by Holabird & Roche on Michigan Avenue, and the Schlesinger & Mayer department store (1899–1903), later owned by Carson Pirie Scott & Company. This building is considered to be among the most beautiful early expressions of steel-frame construction. Among the finest of his tall office buildings are the

Wainwright, in St. Louis, and the Guaranty, in Buffalo. He had some Chicago residential commissions, including the James Charnley house and a house for his brother Albert. The small bank buildings Sullivan designed throughout the Midwest later in his career are considered comparable to his finest early commissions. In his later years, owing to lack of work and poor health, Sullivan's main effort focused on the writing of *Autobiography of an Idea* (1924) and *A System of Architectural Ornament* (1924).

THEODORE VIGO WADSKIER (1827–1897)

Theodore Wadskier was born on the island of St. Croix in the Danish West Indies. He was educated in Copenhagen and studied architecture at the Royal Academy of Fine Arts there. In 1850, he immigrated to the United States, working first in New York and then in Philadelphia, where he practiced architecture and taught drawing. In 1852 he formed a partnership, Nicholson & Wadskier. That same year, he published *The Practical Sculptor, Comprising a Series of Original Drawings for Monuments, Mantles, Balustrades, & Adapted to the Present Taste and Style of Architecture.*

In 1857, Wadskier moved to Chicago, where he established a practice designing schools, office buildings, churches, and residences. In 1869, he designed the Unity Church, which was one of the costliest buildings in the city, described at the time as one of its most elegant. The church's exterior limestone survived the 1871 Chicago fire, and the structure was rebuilt, later housing the Scottish Rite Cathedral, which still stands, on North Dearborn Street. Wadskier lost everything he owned in the fire of 1871 but reestablished his practice, forming a partnership in 1872 with his nephew Henry Harned, who had moved to

Chicago from Philadelphia that year. Harned took over the practice when Wadskier retired.

PETER BONNETT WIGHT (1836–1925) DRAKE AND WIGHT

P. B. Wight was born in New York. In 1855, he graduated from the Free Academy (later the New York City College) in New York and remained in the city to apprentice with architect Thomas R. Jackson. He took a job in Chicago from 1858 to 1859 with the firm of Carter & Bauer and then returned to New York to work for the architect and architectural critic Russell Sturgis. In 1861, he won a design competition for the National Academy of Design in New York and in 1862 opened his own practice. The National Academy building was influential in introducing High Victorian Gothic architecture to America.

In 1871, following the Chicago fire, Wight moved back to Chicago to take part in the rebuilding of the city, working with Asher Carter and William Drake. He was made their partner and the firm became Carter, Drake and Wight until 1871 when Carter retired. Wight practiced as Drake and Wight until 1875-76 when the partners pursued separate practices. In 1873, he supervised the construction of H. H. Richardson's first Chicago commission, the American Express Building. Among his works were Street Hall at Yale University (1864–66); the Brooklyn Mercantile Library (1867–69); the Springer Block, Chicago (1888), extensively altered by Adler & Sullivan; and the Homeopathic Hospital at the 1893 World's Fair. This building had an arched entryway remarkably similar to the entrance on Sullivan's Transportation Building at the Fair. Wight's work was influenced by that of A. W. N. Pugin, who was responsible for initiating the Gothic Revival style in England. In addition to buildings, Wight designed furniture and wallpaper and decorated interiors with ornamental patternwork in the style of another influential English designer, Owen Jones.

Wight was an innovator in the field of fireproof construction. In 1874, he patented a fireproof, concrete-clad iron column and in 1878, he patented the design for a tile arch ceiling that fireproofed floor construction. Wight founded the Wight Fireproofing Company, which was responsible for the fireproofing of several hundred buildings, including William Le Baron Jenney's Home Insurance Building (1884), Chicago's first steel-frame skyscraper.

From the 1890s on, Wight wrote articles for all the major architectural journals, establishing a national reputation as an author and architectural critic.

FRANK LLOYD WRIGHT (1867–1959)

Frank Lloyd Wright is arguably America's most famous architect of the first half of the 20th century. His professional career covered 70 years, during which he built over 300 buildings. As with other great 20th-century architects with long careers, Wright's architecture developed and changed. In his early and most innovative period, spent working in Chicago and its suburbs, he produced a body of Prairie style work that had an important impact on the development of 20th-century European modern architecture. Throughout his career, Wright built important religious, civic, and commercial structures, including Unity Temple in Oak Park, Illinois (1906), the Larkin Building in Buffalo, New York (1904), the Johnson Wax Building in Racine, Wisconsin (1936–46), and the Guggenheim Museum in New York City (completed after his death in 1959).

Wright made his greatest mark and did his most important work as a residential architect. He worked in the Chicago area from 1887 to 1909, and during this time he developed a language of highly original residential architecture by reinventing, transforming, and abstracting the elements of the traditional house. He understood interior space and its visual relationship to the exterior in a new way that stressed the spatial connections between rooms and also between inside spaces and outdoor porches and terraces. Wright's work, and the work of Chicago architects that he influenced, came to be known as the Prairie School of architecture.

Wright was born in 1867 in Richland Center, Wisconsin. His father William, a New England clergyman, settled the family in Madison, Wisconsin when Wright was 11. They lived near the family of Wright's mother, the Lloyd Joneses, who were Welsh Unitarian farmers. His father abandoned his family and Wright never finished high school, although he spent one semester as a special student at the University of Wisconsin in the engineering department. Through a recommendation from his uncle, Jenkin Lloyd Jones, he went to work in the Chicago office of Joseph Lyman Silsbee. Silsbee had designed a small Unitarian chapel for Wright's uncle and took the young man on as an apprentice. From Silsbee's office, Wright went to work for Louis Sullivan. He was employed by Adler & Sullivan from 1888 to 1893, during which time he was put in charge of the residential commissions in the office.

In 1889, Wright married and, with Sullivan's help, bought property in Oak Park, where he designed and built a fashionable Shingle style house like those he had worked on in Silsbee's office. Wright also designed residences for friends in Oak Park, but because this was in violation of his contract with Sullivan, he was fired. Wright set up his own practice in Chicago, working with his friend Cecil Corwin and sharing space with Dwight Perkins in Steinway Hall. In 1895, he added an office and studio to his house in Oak Park and moved his practice there, hiring Walter Burley Griffin and Marion Mahony Griffin, John Van Bergen, William Drummond, and Barry Byrne to work with him. Important residential commissions from this period included the Ward Willits house in Highland Park (1902), the Darwin Martin house in Buffalo, New York (1904), the Avery Coonley house in River Forest (1908), and the Frederick Robie house in Chicago (1909).

In 1909, Wright left his family in Chicago to go to Berlin with the wife of his client Edwin Cheney, with whom he was having an affair. The purpose of the trip was to arrange for the publication of a portfolio of drawings of his work to be issued by the Berlin publisher Ernst Wasmuth. The Wasmuth Portfolio greatly enhanced Wright's growing international reputation at a time when his life was in shambles. His wife refused to give him a divorce, and the growing scandal caused by his departure for Europe with Mrs. Cheney effectively ended his career in Chicago. Wright moved on, building a new residence and studio in 1911 on farm property his mother owned near Spring Green, Wisconsin.

BIBLIOGRAPHY

GENERAL REFERENCES

American Institute of Architects. *American Architects Directory*. 2nd ed. New York: R. R. Bowker, 1962.

The Book of Chicagoans. Chicago: A. N. Marquis, 1905, 1911, 1917, and 1926.

Handbook for Architects and Builders. Chicago: Illinois Society of Architects, 1898–c. 1935.

Who's Who in Chicago. Chicago: A. N. Marquis, 1931.

Who's Who in Chicago and Vicinity. Chicago: A. N. Marquis, 1936 and 1941.

Withey, Henry F., and Elsie Rathburn. *Biographical Dictionary of American Architects (Deceased)*. Los Angeles: Hennessey and Ingalls, 1970.

PERIODICALS AND NEWSPAPERS

American Architect and Building News. Boston and New York, 1876–1938.

The Architect. New York, 1910–32.

The Architectural Forum; Brickbuilder. New York, 1896–1924.

The Architectural Record. New York, 1891–1932.

The Architectural Review. Boston, 1891–1921.

Architecture. New York, 1900–1930.

Chicago Daily News.

Chicago Tribune.

George W. Maher Quarterly. Sauk City, Wisconsin.

House and Garden. Chicago and New York. 1901–93; 1996–present.

House Beautiful. New York, 1896–present.

Inland Architect and News Record. Chicago, 1889–1908.

Prairie School Review. Chicago, 1964–81.

Town and Country. New York, 1846–present.

Western Architect. Minneapolis, 1902–31.

BOOKS, PRINTED MATERIAL, AND ARTICLES

Angle, Paul M. *The Great Chicago Fire: Described in Seven Letters by Men and Women Who Experienced Its Horrors, and Now Published in Commemoration of the Seventy-Fifth Anniversary of the Catastrophe*. Chicago: Chicago Historical Society, 1946.

Ascoli, Peter M. *Julius Rosenwald: The Man Who Built Sears, Roebuck and Advanced the Cause of Black Education in the American South*. Bloomington and Indianapolis: Indiana University Press, 2006.

Banks, Charles Eugene. *Beautiful Homes and Social Customs of America*. Chicago: Bible Publishers, 1902.

Beadle, Muriel, and the Centennial History Committee. *The Fortnightly of Chicago: The City and Its Women, 1873–1973*. Chicago: Henry Regnery, 1973.

Berger, Miles. *They Built Chicago*. Chicago: Bonus Books, 1992.

Betsky, Aaron. *James Gamble Rogers and the Architecture of Pragmatism*. Cambridge: The MIT Press, 1994.

The Biographical Dictionary and Portrait Gallery of Representative Men of Chicago, St. Louis and the World's Columbian Exposition. Chicago and New York: American Biographical Publishing, 1893.

Block, Jean F. *Hyde Park Houses: An Informal History, 1856–1910.* Chicago: University of Chicago Press, 1978.

Brooks, H. Allen. *The Prairie School: Frank Lloyd Wright and His Midwest Contemporaries.* Toronto: University of Toronto Press, 1972.

Bruegmann, Robert. *Holabird & Roche, Holabird and Root: An Illustrated Catalogue of Works.* 3 vols. New York: Garland, in cooperation with Chicago Historical Society, 1991.

Busch, Akiko. *Geography of Home.* New York: Princeton Architectural Press, 1999.

Chatfield-Taylor, H. C., with illustrations by Lester G. Hornby. *Chicago.* New York: Houghton Mifflin, 1917.

Chicago's Accomplishments and Leaders. Chicago: Bishop, 1932.

Chicago Historic Resources Survey: An Inventory of Architecturally and Historically Significant Structures. Chicago: Commission on Chicago Landmarks and the Chicago Department of Planning and Development, 1996.

Cigliano, Jan, and Sarah Bradford Landau, eds. *The Grand American Avenue: 1850–1920.* San Francisco: Pomegranate Artbooks, in association with The Octagon: The Museum of the American Architectural Foundation, 1995.

Clark, Herma. *The Elegant Eighties: When Chicago Was Young.* With a foreword by John T. McCutcheon. Chicago: A. S. McClurg, 1941.

Conners, Joseph. *The Robie House of Frank Lloyd Wright.* Chicago: University of Chicago Press, 1984.

Coorens, Elaine A. *Wicker Park: From 1673 thru 1929 and Walking Tour Guide.* Chicago: Old Wicker Park Committee, 2003.

Coventry, Kim, Daniel Meyer, and Arthur H. Miller. *Classic Country Estates of Lake Forest: Architecture and Landscape Design, 1856–1940.* New York: Norton, 2003.

Cronon, William. *Nature's Metropolis: Chicago and the Great West.* New York: Norton, 1991.

Dedmon, Emmett. *Fabulous Chicago.* New York: Random House, 1953.

Drury, John. *Old Chicago Houses: 110 Stately Landmarks and Their Stories.* New York: Bonanza Books, 1941.

The Early Work of Frank Lloyd Wright: The "Ausgefhrte Bauten" of 1911. New York: Dover, 1982.

Eaton, Leonard K. *Two Chicago Architects and Their Clients: Frank Lloyd Wright and Howard Van Doren Shaw.* Cambridge: MIT Press, 1969.

Edgren, Gretchen. *Inside the Playboy Mansion: If You Don't Swing, Don't Ring.* London: Aurum Press, 1998.

Farr, Finis. *Chicago: A Personal History of America's Most American City.* New Rochelle, N.Y.: Arlington House, 1973.

Garden, Hugh M. G. "The Chicago School." *The Prairie School Review.* Vol. 3. First Quarter, 1966.

Gilbert, Paul, and Charles Lee Bryson. *Chicago and Its Makers.* Chicago: Felix Mendelsohn, 1929.

Graf, John. *Chicago's Mansions.* Chicago: Arcadia, 2004.

Granger, Alfred. *Chicago Welcomes You.* Chicago: A. Kroch, 1933.

Green, Virginia. *The Architecture of Howard Van Doren Shaw.* Chicago: Chicago Review Press, 1998.

Greengard, B. C. "Hugh M. G. Garden." *The Prairie School Review.* Vol. 3. First Quarter, 1966.

Grossman, James R., Ann Durkin Keating, and Janice L. Reiff, eds. *The Encyclopedia of Chicago.* Chicago: University of Chicago Press, 2004.

Harrington, Elaine. *Henry Hobson Richardson: J. J. Glessner House, Chicago.* Berlin: Ernst Wasmuth Verlag, 1993.

Harrison, Carter H., Jr. *Growing Up with Chicago.* Chicago: Ralph Fletcher Seymour, 1944.

Hasbrouck, Wilbert R. *The Chicago Architectural Club: Prelude to the Modern.* New York: Monacelli Press, 2005.

Hayes, Dorsha B. *Chicago: Crossroads of American Enterprise.* New York: Julian Messner, 1944.

Hitchcock, Henry-Russell. *The Architecture of H. H. Richardson and His Times.* New York: Museum of Modern Art, 1936.

Hoffman, Donald. *The Architecture of John Wellborn Root.* Baltimore: The John Hopkins University Press, 1973.

Hoffman, Donald. *Frank Lloyd Wright's Robie House: The Illustrated Story of an Architectural Masterpiece.* New York: Dover, 1984.

Hoffman, Donald, ed. *The Meanings of Architecture: Buildings and Writings by John Wellborn Root.* New York: Horizon Press, 1967.

Horowitz, Helen Lefkowitz. *Culture & the City: Cultural Philanthropy in Chicago from the 1880s to 1917.* Chicago: University of Chicago Press, 1976.

Jaher, Frederic Cople. *The Urban Establishment: Upper Strata in Boston, New York, Charleston, Chicago, and Los Angeles.* Urbana, Ill.: University of Chicago Press, 1982.

Jones, John H., and Fred Britten, eds. *A Half Century of Chicago Building.* Chicago: n.p., 1910.

Kilner, Collen Browne. *Joseph Sears and his Kenilworth.* Kenilworth: Kenilworth Historical Society, 1990.

Kirkfleet, Rev. Cornelius J. *The Life of Patrick Augustine Feehan, Bishop of Nashville, First Archbishop of Chicago.* Chicago: Matre, 1922.

Kirkland, Caroline. *Chicago Yesterdays: A Sheaf of Reminiscences.* Chicago: Daughaday, 1919.

Landau, Sarah Bradford. *P. B. Wight: Architect, Contractor, and Critic, 1838–1925.* Chicago: Art Institute of Chicago, 1981.

Lewis, Arnold, James Turner, and Steven McQuillin. *The Opulent Interiors of the Gilded Age.* New York: Dover, 1987.

Longstreth, Richard, ed. *The Charnley House.* Chicago: University of Chicago Press, 2004.

Lowe, David. *Chicago Interiors: Views of a Splendid World.* Chicago: Contemporary Books, 1979.

———. *Lost Chicago.* Boston: Houghton Mifflin, 1975.

Maher, Virginia Jones. "George M. Niedecken: The Search for an American Design Style." *Wisconsin Academy Review* 43 (Summer 1997), accessed online.

Manson, Grant Carpenter. *Frank Lloyd Wright to 1910: The First Golden Age.* New York: Van Nostrand Reinhold, 1958.

Mayer, Harold M., and Richard C. Wade. *Chicago: Birth of a Metropolis.* Chicago: University of Chicago Press, 1969.

McCarthy, Kathleen D. *Noblesse Oblige: Charity & Cultural Philanthropy in Chicago, 1849–1929.* Chicago: University of Chicago Press, 1982.

Meeker, Arthur. *Chicago with Love: A Polite and Personal History.* New York: Knopf, 1955.

———. *Prairie Avenue.* New York: Knopf, 1949.

Molloy, Mary Alice, "Prairie Avenue, Chicago, Illinois" in *The Grand American Avenue: 1850–1920*, ed., Jan Cigliano and Sarah Bradford Landau. San Francisco: Pomegranate Artbooks, 1994.

Monroe, Harriet. *John Wellborn Root.* Boston: Houghton Mifflin, 1896.

Morgan, Joan, and Alison Richards. *A Paradise out of a Common Field: The Pleasures and Plenty of the Victorian Gardens.* New York: Harper & Row, 1990.

Morrison, Hugh. *Louis Sullivan, Prophet of Modern Architecture.* New York: Norton, 1935.

Ochsner, Jeffrey Karl. *H. H. Richardson, Complete Architectural Works.* Cambridge, Mass.: MIT Press, 1982.

O'Gorman, James F. *H. H. Richardson. Architectural*

forms for an American Society. Chicago: The University of Chicago Press, 1987.

O'Gorman, James. *Selected Drawings, H. H. Richardson and His Office.* Harvard College Library, 1974.

Pictorial Chicago and Illustrated World's Columbian Exposition. Chicago: Rand McNally, 1893.

Pierce, Bessie Louise. *A History of Chicago, Volume III: The Rise of a Modern City, 1871–1893.* Chicago: University of Chicago Press, 1957.

Roth, Leland M. *The Architecture of McKim, Mead and White, 1870–1920: A Building List.* New York: Garland, 1978.

Rudd, J. William, comp. *Historic American Buildings Survey: Chicago and Nearby Areas.* Park Forest, Ill.: Prairie School Press, 1966.

Salny, Stephen M. *The Country Houses of David Adler.* New York: Norton, 2001.

Sheldon, George William. *Artistic Country Seats, Volume 1.* New York: D. Appleton and Company, 1886. reprinted, New York: Da Capo Press, Inc., 1979.

Schultz, Rima Lunin, and Adele Hast, eds. *Women Building Chicago, 1790–1990.* Bloomington and Indianapolis: Indiana University Press, 2001.

Schulze, Franz, and Kevin Harrington. *Chicago's Famous Buildings: A Photographic Guide to the City's Architectural Landmarks and Other Notable Buildings.* Chicago: University of Chicago Press, 1993.

Sinkevitch, Alice, ed. *AIA Guide to Chicago.* Joint venture of the American Institute of Architects, Chicago; Chicago Architecture Foundation; Landmarks Preservation Council of Illinois and the Commission on Chicago Landmarks. New York: Harcourt Brace, 2004.

Spears, Timothy B. *Chicago Dreaming: Midwesterners and the City, 1871–1919.* Chicago: University of Chicago Press, 1905.

Spencer, Brian A., ed. *The Prairie School Tradition: The Prairie Archives of the Milwaukee Art Center.* New York: Whitney Library of Design, 1985.

Stamper, John W. *Chicago's North Michigan Avenue: Planning and Development, 1900–1930.* Chicago: University of Chicago Press, 1991.

Tallmadge, Thomas Eddy. *Architecture in Old Chicago.* Chicago: University of Chicago Press, 1941.

Thorne, Martha, ed. *David Adler, Architect: The Elements of Style.* New Haven, Conn.: Art Institute of Chicago in association with Yale University Press, 2002.

Van Rensselaer, Marianna Griswold. *Henry Hobson Richardson and His Works.* Houghton, Mifflin & Company, 1888.

Van Zanten, David. *Sullivan's City.* New York: Norton, 2000.

West, James L. W., II. *The Perfect Hour: The Romance of F. Scott Fitzgerald and Ginevra King, His First Love.* New York: Random House, 2005.

Westfall, C. W. "From Homes to Towers: A Century of Chicago's Best Hotels and Tall Apartment Buildings." In John Zukowsky, ed., *Chicago Architecture, 1872–1922: Birth of a Metropolis.* Munich: Prestel-Verlag, in association with the Art Institute of Chicago, 1987.

Who's Who of American Women (and Women of Canada): A Biographical Dictionary of Notable Living Women of the United States of America and Other Countries. 5th ed., 1968–69. Chicago: A. N. Marquis, 1969.

Zorbaugh, Harvey Warren. *The Gold Coast and the Slum: A Sociological Study of Chicago's Near North Side.* Chicago: University of Chicago Press, 1929. Repr. 1976.

UNPUBLISHED AND PRIVATELY PRINTED MATERIAL

"The Astor Street District." Chicago: Commission on Chicago Historical and Architectural Landmarks, 1976.

Blatchford, Charles Hammond, Jr. *Eliphalet W. Blatchford & Mary E. Blatchford: The Story of Two Chicagoans.* Chicago: Privately printed, 1962.

Blatchford Family Papers, Additions, 1835–1948. Chicago: The Newberry Library.

"The Bryan Lathrop House: Historic Structures Report." Chicago: T. Gunny Harboe, AIA, director, McClier Preservation Group, May 1998.

Commission on Chicago Historical and Architectural Landmarks. *Alta Vista Terrace Landmark District*. Chicago, n.d. Bound pamphlet.

"The Fortnightly of Chicago: A Social Architectural History" Chicago. From the notes of Patricia Cooper Kubicek, March 2000.

Glessner, John J. "The Story of a house." unpublished, 1923. Quoted in Harrington, *Henry Hobson Richardson : J. J. Glessner House, Chicago*.

Henrietta and Fred Whiting. *The House that was Home*. Fairfield: Fairfield Graphic Inc. May 7, 1987. Memoir of Eleanor Robinson Countiss Whiting and her home.

"Kenwood District." Chicago: Commission on Chicago Historical and Architectural Landmarks, 1978.

Love, Richard H., and Michael Preston Worley. "The Samuel M. Nickerson House of Chicago: Neo-Renaissance Palazzo and Private Art Gallery of the Gilded Age." Chicago: R. H. Love Galleries, 1998.

Madlener House: Tradition and Innovation in Architecture. Chicago: Graham Foundation, 1988.

"McCormick Double House," 660 North Rush Street. Landmark Designation Report: Commission on Chicago Landmarks, Department of Development and Planning, City of Chicago, 2004.

Notz, John K., Jr. "To Cathect or Not to Cathect." Paper delivered to the Chicago Literary Club, March 11, 1996 (http://www.shilit.org/NOTZ1.HTM).

Rudd, J. William. *George W. Maher-Architect*. Unpublished Masters Thesis.Chicago: Northwestern University, 1964.

"Samuel M. Nickerson House," Chicago: Commission on Chicago Historical and Architectural Landmarks, 1977.

Uihlein, Edward Gustav (1845–1921). "Memories of My Youth," 1917ff. Transcribed from German by Rosina Laurette Lippi and others, under the auspices of John K. Notz Jr., 1905.

ILLUSTRATION CREDITS

American Architect and Building News: (Feb. 26, 1881) 101, (December, 1892) 167

American College of Surgeons: 98, 99, 100

Archdiocese of Chicago Archives and Records Center: 129, 130 top and bottom

Architectural Forum: (April 1922): 266, 267, 268 top and bottom, 269, 270

Architectural Record: (Vol. VI, July 1896-June 1897, p. 84) 104, (XVII No. 6, June 1905., p. 491-8): 212, 213, 215, 216 top and bottom, (Vol. XVIII, Aug. 1905) 218, 223, (XVIII No. 1, July 1905) 226, 227, 228, 229 top and bottom, 230, 231, 232, (Feb. 1896 Great American Architect Series, No. 2) 296 middle left

Art Institute of Chicago, Historic Architecture and Landscape Image Collection, Ryerson and Burnham Archives: 16, 36, 46, 47, 50, 61, 62, 90, 91, 92, 94, 95, 96, 97, 118, 119, 120, 121, 122, 123, 124 top and bottom, 126, 135, 148, 149, 152, 154, 155, 156, 157, 158, 159, 162, 163, 164, 165 top and bottom, 166, 174, 214, 233, 240, 241, 242, 243, 247, 271, 290 top and bottom, 291 top and bottom, 293 top right and bottom left, 294 top right, middle left and right, bottom right, 295 middle left and right, 296 middle right and bottom left, 297 top right and bottom left and right

Artistic Country Seats: 127

Ausgefuhrte Bauten und Entwurfe von Frank Lloyd Wright, Berlin: Verlag Ernst Wasmuth, 1910: 248 bottom, 297 middle left

Beautiful Homes and Social Customs of America: 112, 113, 114, 115

Cohen and Hacker Architects LLC, courtesy of: 160, 256, 257

Charnley-Persky House Museum: 102, 128

Chicago and its Makers: 19, 45

Chicago Architectural Club Annual, 1930: 26

Chicago Historical Museum: 14, 20, 21, 22 left and right, 25, 27, 60, 64, 65, 66 top and bottom, 67, 68, 69, 76, 82, 83, 89, 103, 105 top and bottom, 106, 107, 108, 110, 111, 125, 136, 176, 177 left, 177 right, 184 top, 184 bottom, 185 top and bottom, 187, 193, 197, 198, 199 top, 204, 205, 206, 207 top and bottom, 208, 209, 210, 211 top and bottom, 250, 251, 252 top and bottom, 253, 254, 255, 274, 275, 276 top and bottom, 277, 279, 280, 282, 283, 284, 285, 286, 287, 288, 289, 292 top left and bottom right and left, 293 middle left and right, 294 top right and bottom left, 295 top right and bottom left and right, 296 top right and bottom right, 298 top left, middle right, and bottom right, frontis

Chicago With Love: 87

Eifler, John, Courtesy of: 173

Frank Lloyd Wright Preservation Trust: 248 top

Glessner House Museum: 88, 117, 139, 140, 141 top and bottom, 142, 143, 144, 147, 293 top left, 297 middle right

Hedrich Blessing (photos by Nick Merrick): 168, 169, 170, 171

Henry Hobson Richardson and His Works, 153, 161

Historic American Buildings Survey: 149, 150, 192, 195, 196, 199 bottom, 235 right, 239

INDEX